Women's Agency
and
Educational Policy

SUNY series, The Social Context of Education
Christine E. Sleeter, editor

Women's Agency and Educational Policy

The Experiences of the Women of Kilome, Kenya

mutindi mumbua kiluva-ndunda

STATE UNIVERSITY OF NEW YORK PRESS

Published by
State University of New York Press, Albany

For information, address the State University of New York Press
90 State Street, Suite 700, Albany, NY 12207

Production by Kristin Milavec
Marketing by Anne M. Valentine

Library of Congress Cataloging-in-Publication Data

Kiluva-Ndunda, Mutindi Mumbua.
    Women's agency and educational policy : the experiences of the
women of Kilome, Kenya / Mutindi Mumbua Kiluva-Ndunda.
        p.   cm. — (SUNY series, the social context of education)
    Includes bibliographical references (p.) and index.
    ISBN 0-7914-4761-8 (alk. paper)—ISBN 0-7914-4762-6 (pbk. : alk. paper)
        1. Women—Education—Social aspects—Kenya—Kilome.   2. Education
and state—Kenya—Kilome.   3. Women—Kenya—Kilome—Social
conditions.   4. Kilome (Kenya).   I. Title.   II. SUNY series, social
context of education.

    LC2474.2 .K54   2001
    305.42'096762—dc21   00-020576
                                                              CIP

10 9 8 7 6 5 4 3 2 1

Contents

Preface

T his book is about women's perception of education and the sacrifices they make to afford their children meaningful educational opportunities. It focuses on the educational experiences of the women of Kilome, Kenya. Contrary to the public discourse on the education of women articulated in Kenyan policy documents, women's private discourses on education emphasize higher education as the key to self-reliance for their children.

The sacrifices that women make to achieve higher education are many. For me, the ultimate sacrifice was leaving my two young children—a two year old and a three year old—to pursue a master's degree in Canada. The joy of winning a prestigious Canadian International Development Agency (CIDA) scholarship was shrouded by the reality of this sacrifice.

It was very difficult for me to reconcile the contradictions of motherhood and the development of my career. For a woman to leave her young children to pursue her education abroad was a choice that few Kenyan men and women accepted. However, growing up in a polygamous home, I knew how important it was for a woman to have something that she could call her own: Education was that "something" that could give a woman economic independence. I decided to develop my career unlike my mother, who was compelled to support my father's career development only to lose control over the benefits of his career when he became a "modern polygamist." Traditionally, the first wife chose her cowife/wives and had control over the family's resources.

The journey of my education begins with my mother, who like many mothers in my village, valued the education of all her children irrespective of their gender. She enrolled me in school when I became of age and made sure that I was fed, clean, and had all the resources I needed to learn. She provided the material labor that I required so that I could succeed in school. The journey of my schooling continues with my brother, who became a crucial intervention agent when he forfeited his scholarship to study international law. He worked so that he could pay my school fees in a prestigious former European girls-only high school.

This book presents the voices of women of Kilome, who like my mother, make untold sacrifices to educate their children. Most of them were denied educational opportunities by their fathers who did not value the education of women. These women were not as lucky as I was to have an intervention agent. However, the women desperately want to give their daughters high-level educational opportunities. They have engaged in strenuous multiple income-generating activities to afford their children educational and economic opportunities. The women speak of "sacrificing" themselves for their children even though many of these women are physically ill. The women's stories are told with sensitivity, treading gently, like the chameleon, careful not to create another "discourse of horror" (Roman, personal communication, 1992) about anonymous "subjects" of study.

These women have become crucial intervention agents for their children, and in particular, for their daughters. As agents of change, the women know that the way things are is neither inevitable nor immutable. The intent of this book is to highlight women's agency as well as their struggles to afford their children educational opportunities. The women's narratives make visible their agency and their compliance. The implementation of educational and development policies such as the structural adjustment policies has exacerbated the demand for women's labor within the social, economic and political context of Kenyan society. As we shall see, this social crisis has impacted negatively on the education and health of women.

This work has come a long way since I completed my fieldwork in 1994 and completed writing my Ph.D. dissertation in 1995. There are many who have contributed to the richness of my intellectual and personal development. I am greatly indebted to the International Development Research Centre (IDRC) for funding my fieldwork in Kenya. Without their financial support, Kilome women's experiences and struggles would continue to remain hidden.

I would like to thank Hugh Munby for helping me to understand the importance of having passion. I thank Magda Lewis for opening my eyes to feminist discourses. It was in her class where

I began to understand the nature of women's oppression. I thank Tom Russell, and Glen and Shirley Eastabrook for caring for me and my family while we were in Canada.

I would like to thank Jane Gaskell, Leslie Roman, Jean Barman, and Deirdre Kelly for their guidance and support during my graduate program. I am indebted to Jean Barman for her enthusiasm, insights, love, kindness, and support. She was there to dispel my fears and has continued to be a bridge for me.

My very sincere thanks go to Christine Sleeter. Without her, this work would be collecting dust somewhere, forgotten. The women of Kilome and I are indebted to her for intervening for us. Her commitment to inclusionary practices provided me with the shoulders on which to stand.

I am grateful to my friends and colleagues at the College of Charleston and specifically, in the School of Education. They have enriched me in many ways. Special thanks go to Meta Van Sickle, Mary Blake, Angela Cozart, Angela Bolden, Fran Courson, Jeri Cabot, Diane Cudahy, Bob Fowler, Linda Fitzharris, Monica Janas, Christine Finnan, Bob Perkins, Nancy Sorenson, Mike Skinner, Nancy Waller, and Frances Welch. I want to thank Ford Walpole very much for editing my work. I am truly grateful for the sacrifices he made for me and for sticking with me to the end. Many thanks to Eric and Kathryn Treml for "rescuing" the research sites' map project at the eleventh hour!

I am grateful to Cactus Press and to Vincent R. D'Oyley for allowing me to quote from the chapter entitled "Women's Struggle for Education: Private and Public Discourses on Education in Kenya" in *Re/Visioning: Canadian Perspectives on the Education of Africans in the Late Twentieth Century* by Vincent R. D'Oyley and E. James (1998).

I am indebted to my family for their support and encouragement throughout my academic journey. To my mother, you are a wonderful woman. Your courage and grace have carried us through stormy periods. To my brother Fred, you are my hero. Thank you for giving up your career for me. Mumo, thank you for your strength and courage. To my husband, Thomas Ndunda, you gave up so much so that you could be with your family. We are all so grateful. To my children, Nthenya and Ndambuki, thank you for letting me share with the world the experiences of the women of our village. I hope I have been a good role model for you.

This book speaks with the voices of the women of Kilome who opened up their hearts to share their stories with me. I want you to know that I continue to feel the pain and the anger of your experiences, which still bring tears to my eyes. However, I am encouraged by your determination—by your agency. I dedicate this book to you and to your daughters. May we continue to open doors for each other!

1

Introduction

Main Focus

This book is about women's perceptions of the uses of education in Kenya. It focuses on rural women's experiences of formal education in Kilome division, Makueni District, Kenya. The purpose of the study, which this book is based on, was to clarify the cultural, historical, social, economic, and political factors that have shaped and continue to shape women's educational and employment opportunities. Specifically, the study sought to highlight Kilome women's agency[1] in their struggle to offer their children—particularly their daughters—educational and economic opportunities.

My interest in a study of women's experiences of education and in Kilome division in particular, arose largely from my own experience growing up in this area. Mothers, most of whom were de facto heads of households, played a key role in the welfare and education of their children. They provided the material labor required to maintain their children in school, especially at the primary level (grades 1–7 or 8). In my case, I do not remember any one time when my father was able to attend the weekly parents' work sessions at school. (Parents fetched water and made bricks for building classrooms.) It was my mother who came to school to work and bought me the stationery I needed. She was the one who made sure I was in school when I was supposed to be. Women were overrepresented in the Wednesday parents' school work sessions. Nevertheless, these women's struggles to afford their children educational opportunities have not been acknowledged. Their struggles are shaped by the social, economic, and political contexts within which they operate.

1

To understand the women's contexts, it became important to understand their own educational journeys. The women narrated their stories in relation to education highlighting their experiences of formal education and the constraints they have faced, and continue to face, in Kenya today. Their narratives expose and draw attention to the gender and power issues that limit their participation in education and in the formal employment sector, issues that in general, exacerbate gender inequalities and the subordination of women individually and collectively. These are issues that policymakers, politicians, development agents, and educators do not adequately address or challenge. The women speak about their experiences from their standpoints.[2] Their material locations are shaped by ethnicity, gender, marital status, age, and region.

The women articulate their experiences relating to education in the past (their own) and in the present (their daughters), highlighting fears and hopes, and possibilities and constraints that structure their daily lives. They also articulate their experiences concerning labor, both paid and unpaid. This makes visible the increasing demand for women's labor as they intervene for their families' welfare within a harsh social, economic, and political climate (George, 1994; Mbilinyi, 1998; Mikell, 1997). The discussion of family and sexuality demonstrates women's perceptions of themselves, of their daughters, and of their roles in the family. The women do not define their agency simply around motherhood in the private sphere. As Stamp (1995) argues, women in rural African communities have multiple subjectivity as mothers, daughters, sisters, traders, and farmers, which is the bedrock of their agency in the Kenyan state today. Women's participation in self-help groups further highlights their collective agency. I construe the women's narratives as their private discourse on education, one that operates in the family and in the community.

I contrast the private discourse with the public discourse on education articulated in policy documents, highlighting the contradictions and similarities between the different narrative standpoints. The public discourse regarding the purpose of education of men and women in Kenya is set out by male politicians, policy makers, and international development agencies such as the World Bank. I analyzed educational and development related policy documents[3] produced over the last thirty-year period to document the public discourse. Analysis of national development plans is important because education is viewed as an instrument of national development. The analysis of the private and public discourse on education makes visible women's agency and the systemic gender discrimination that women face in accessing educational and economic opportunities in Kenya.

Background

Education occupies a central position in the national development plans of many countries, including Kenya. Since independence in 1963, the government has set up several commissions and working parties to look into ways and means of structuring and restructuring education to meet the country's development needs and more importantly, to meet international financiers[4] demands. They have recommended policies that have served to shape education and educational opportunities in Kenya. While women constitute over 50% of the population of Kenya, gender issues that limit their participation in education and in the economy have consistently remained invisible to policy makers. This has maintained the low representation of women in all levels of education and in the labor market, since educational qualifications are used as criteria for hiring for employment in most areas in the modern sector. The commissions that have been set up have emphasized the economic, rather than the social function of education.

Although the public discourse on education has expressed a commitment to providing education to all Kenyans, absent in this policy discourse has been the discussion of how gender has influenced opportunities available to men and women in colonial and post-colonial Kenya. Gender is a social, cultural, economic, and political construction of what it means to be a girl or a boy, or a woman or a man in a given context.[5] It is a social process that ascribes characteristics and behaviors to women and men according to their sex (Eyre, 1993). Gender constructions of femininity have continued to limit educational opportunities made available to women in postcolonial Kenya.

In Kenya, men play a dominant role in all aspects of governance. Kenyan women have had difficulty penetrating the patriarchal decision-making structures and processes of the state and the party. Policy making, planning and development, and implementation of policies and programs in Kenya usually take the male perspective (Kibwana, 1992). The failure to address the impact of seemingly gender-neutral educational policies has reinforced gender inequities in educational opportunities, for instance, the implementation of the cost-sharing strategy, where parents have to pay for schooling, has increased women's work loads and intensified their daughters' struggles for educational opportunities. The interplay between gendered cultural assumptions about femininity and the increased costs of schooling have a negative impact on women's education.

The formulation of policies from the male perspective also intensifies the public and private dichotomy[6] on the basis of gender. Policy makers seem to confine the discourse on women's education to their agency in the private sphere. They do not view women as economic and political agents in the public sphere alongside men. This has led to the formulation of policies that have served to reinforce gender inequities in the public sphere. This thesis proceeds on the assumption that gender and power issues must be taken as fundamental categories within which human social relations are organized (Harding, 1986).

The government of Kenya professes to be committed to the provision of equal opportunities to all of its citizens irrespective of sex, race, and religion. The government also claims to be committed to addressing the unequal social, economic, and political status of women in Kenya. However, in reality, the government is resistant to gender issues, for example, women, who have voiced and articulated women's concerns, such as Professor Wangari Mathai, have frequently been met with severe and brutal repression. Mathai, the first female professor of veterinary medicine in Kenya, and founder of the world renowned environmental GreenBelt movement, has been arrested numerous times for challenging men's supremacy in making decisions that are gender biased and environmentally destructive. Women who attempt to exercise their political and economic agency in the public sphere are faced with a multitude of limitations. As Mathai observes, gender, marriage and ethnicity (among others) serve to limit women's agency contrary to the popular publicly promoted rhetoric that "the sky is the limit (quoted in Gruduah, 1991)."

As a female child growing up in a polygamous home in rural Kenya, I am aware of the gender and power issues, nestled in cultural beliefs about women that limit women's/girls' educational opportunities in the society. The clear gender division of roles in my family were those of a mother, wife, care giver, and food producer. These were roles that were limited to the private sphere. Women had performed these roles in the precolonial era before the introduction of formal education and continued to learn them informally. On the other hand, the man was the head of the household, though he often spent most of the time in the city as a migrant worker. He was the "breadwinner," the income earner, and the one who made all the decisions that shaped each and every household member's life. Formal education was considered necessary for his economic role. The woman's unpaid labor, though crucial to the survival of the family, was not as valued as the paid work performed by the man.

About 50% of the girls who enrolled in the first year of primary level education (Standard 1) with me left school before completing this level to become mothers and/or wives or to work as domestic help. Less than 30% of the girls passed the secondary entry examinations, and even fewer completed that level. Only three of us completed the tertiary level of education. I am, therefore, personally aware of how gender and power factors shape women's educational and economic opportunities within the historical, social, economic, and political context of Kenyan society.

Overview of the Book

Chapter 2 provides an overview of the ways in which gender has structured Kenyan women's participation in education, in the economy, and in the family. It also highlights women's concerted efforts to retain their control of work through individual and group activities—self-help groups. I describe the three research sites in detail in chapter 3. The discussion covers life, schooling, and women's activities in each site. These details enable the reader to see the differences and similarities that exist within the same region and how they shape the lives of the women and their children. The chapter also gives an overview of the participants.

Chapter 4 deals with the methodology of my research. Articulation of the methodology/ies is not only important to the reader but also to researchers because it enables the latter to put into words their seemingly indescribable inner beliefs and assumptions that shape their actions. Finally, I reflect on doing research as both an insider and outsider in Kilome division.

Chapter 5 presents the public discourse on education. This discourse is constructed through the analysis of policy documents to show how policies have implications for the public sphere and to show how they limit women's agency. Chapters 6, 7, 8 present the women's discourses. Chapter 6 presents Kilome women's educational experiences. Chapter 7 deals with cultural-gendered assumptions that limit girls' participation in education. Chapter 8 examines the intensification of women's labor as they struggle to educate their children. This includes an examination of rural women's economic activities within a gendered economy. Chapter 9 deals with women's agency in self-help groups and the potential as well as the limitations of these groups in addressing women's concerns.

Chapter 10 is the conclusion. In this chapter, I contrast the women's private discourse with the public discourse on education emphasizing the contradictions as well as the similarities between the narratives.

2

Education and Women's Equity

⚘ ⚘ ⚘ ⚘

Framing the Context

Equality for women involves education, but not just education. Equal access to basic education is endorsed as a basic human right in the World Declaration on Education for All, and was adopted by the world community in Jomtien, Thailand, in 1990. One of the central objectives of the declaration is the reduction in the current gender gap in education, which James Grant as executive director of UNICEF has described as "gender apartheid" (UNICEF/Government of Kenya [GOK], 1992).

Education can provide the impetus to break down stereotypes that exist toward women in a particular society. Kinnear (1997) argues that education can be a tool for the empowerment of women. It raises women's self-esteem and offers them options in their daily lives. Education, however, is not a benign "good" at every moment of its historical path (Bloch & Vavrus, 1998), and experts disagree on how best to achieve gender equity. Roberston and Berger (1986) argue that basic education enhances the subordination of women because it does not offer them meaningful economic opportunities. Hughes and Mwiria (1989) are advocates for girls' higher education, since it has a greater potential for enhancing equity for Kenyan women in the labor market. Specifically, they note that equity for Kenyan women is elusive if factors that limit their access to scientific and technical skills and that exclude them from important areas of the labor market are not addressed. In the same vein Mbilinyi (1972) argues that without the necessary technical skills and vocational

7

training women will remain unemployed or have access only to the lowest-level jobs.

Gender discrimination, in addition to education, limits women's opportunities in the formal employment sector. Assumptions about appropriate roles and suitable careers for women are used to deny them these opportunities. Women in Kenya, like many of their counterparts elsewhere in the world, do not receive remuneration equivalent to that of men with comparable educational attainment (Kagia, 1985; UNICEF/Government of Kenya [GOK], 1992). The few women who participate in the formal employment sector are concentrated in traditional female occupations characterized by low remuneration, few or no benefits, and little opportunity for advancement. In the 1990s, women were experiencing more difficulties than men in securing work in this sector (International Labour Organization [ILO], 1991). Gendered assumptions shape women's lives in ways that limit their participation in public institutions (education, economy, and politics). Gender determines the way in which power, property, prestige, and educational and employment opportunities are organized, regulated, and distributed. However, women are not a coherent group; rather, they are constituted as women through the complex interaction between class, culture, religion, and other ideological institutions and frameworks. "They are not 'women' a coherent group—solely on the basis of a particular economic system or policy" (Mohanty, 1991, pp. 63–64).

This chapter provides a wider lens for viewing the complex gendered public sphere within which Kenyan and specifically, Kilome women struggle for educational and economic opportunities. Kilome women's discourses speak to the reality of the issues raised here. They strive for equal economic and educational opportunities within a context of gender stratification in which power, property, prestige, and social recognition are organized, regulated, distributed, and given meanings (Ahlberg-Maina, 1991, p. 35).

Women and Education in Kenya

Many proponents of women's education in Kenya argue that education, its functions, structure, and output in relation to women, demonstrates that women have been forgotten, neglected, and discriminated against in the provision of educational opportunities (Gachukia & Nzomo, quoted in UNICEF/GOK, 1993; Riria-Ouko, 1984). Gender inequities in the provision of educational opportunities in Kenya have historical and cultural bases (Mukui, 1985). Formal education was introduced to Kenya by the Christian missionaries in the middle of the nineteenth century. Later, education was developed by the colonial government along gender, racial, and ethnic[1] lines. Colonial education severely restricted the education of Africans and almost totally ignored the education of girls (Kagia, 1985). Colonialists, missionaries, and indigenous people all used gender as a criterion for deciding who would receive formal education. Women were systematically excluded from participation in education and thereby from the modern employment sector as formal education credentials and gender became vital criteria.

Since its independence in 1963, Kenya has made significant progress in providing educational services to all Kenyans. The combined efforts of parents, local communities, government and nongovernmental organizations have resulted in high participation in basic education. The national enrollment[2] rate at the primary level in 1991 was 95% compared to 50% at independence and the enrollment rates of boys and girls in primary school are steadily approaching parity. Kenya follows the 8–4–4 (eight years of primary, four years of secondary, and four years of university education) system of education. Primary education is from Standard 1 (six-years old) to Standard 8 (ages fourteen and above). Most primary schools are coeducational, while most secondary schools continue to be divided by gender. In 1991, girls constituted 48.7% of the total enrollment in primary schools, a gender ratio that has remained constant since 1989. Nevertheless, few girls are completing this level of education. A large number of girls who enroll in Standard 1 drop-out of school before they reach Standard 8, for example, of the 864,593 pupils who enrolled in Standard 1 in 1984, 58.4 % of the girls and 53.6% of the boys left school before completing Standard 8 in 1991 (UNICEF/GOK, 1992; Economic Survey, 1992). Though the statistical difference between the dropout rates among boys and girls are not great, the factors that lead to the high dropout rates among the girls, and the fate of those girls who drop out, are significant. National enrollment rates conceal serious gender, regional, and socioeconomic disparities in enrollment, participation, and achievement (UNICEF/GOK, 1992).

The high dropout rates among girls in the primary level of education are associated with:

a. high pregnancy rates among girls in senior primary levels;

b. high tuition and nontuition fees;

c. cultural and traditional practices such as child bride and nomadic practices;

d. poverty resulting in child labor.

Primary schoolgirls are among the increasing number of adolescent mothers in Kenya. In 1986, 12 girls per 1,000 who were enrolled in the secondary level of education left school due to pregnancy (UNICEF/GOK, 1992), since they are blamed for their condition. Therefore, pregnancy marks the end of formal school for most of these girls.

The increasing cost of education exacerbated by the implementation of the cost-sharing strategy by the government of Kenya has become another major barrier to girls' educational opportunities. The burden of tuition and nontuition fees has been too heavy on most parents in rural areas, forcing them to make choices about who is to be educated and for how long. Often, the choice has been to invest in the education of boys for cultural and economic reasons. Cost-sharing policies have not been implemented with sensitivity to gender concerns to the disadvantage of women and girls at all levels. When poor parents are forced to choose between investing in a male child or a female child, the majority will choose their sons (UNICEF/GOK, 1992, p. 108).

Poverty, as well as gendered cultural beliefs about the role of girls and women in the society also limit girls' educational opportunities. The widespread rural-urban male migration and changing social relations in Kenya have resulted in women becoming de facto heads of households and heads of households who must bear all or a large part of the burden of educating their children. Because female heads of households have limited access to resources such as land on which they could produce foodstuffs to provide for their families, girls from such households are likely to drop out of school. Cubbins (1991) argues that in Kenya, women's economic power increases girls' educational opportunities since "economic power is the strongest determinant of gender-based privilege in a society" (p. 1064).

Girls enjoy a much lower status than boys in the cultural, economic, political, religious, and traditional context that prevails in much of Kenya. Girls are likely to enroll in school late because of a need for child labor and they are likely to be overburdened with household chores, which adversely affect their school performance. Girls who enroll late in school will reach adolescence and puberty at lower primary levels where there is a higher chance of performing poorly or of dropping out of school due to pregnancy or marriage. Hyde (1993) notes that among sub-Saharan countries, Kenya included, factors responsible for the second-class status of women in education include:

Ideas about the appropriate roles for women in the labor market or in society, about the biological unsuitability of women for science, and about the gender-based division of work in the household and on the farm influence decisions about schooling as do income, class, religion, and rural or urban residence. (P. 108)

Girls are more likely than boys to be withdrawn from school by their parents to help with household chores or to render services as maids (child laborers) to help feed their families. In addition, young girls are married off as child brides to elderly men for bridewealth; part of which usually finances the education of male siblings. Laws that prohibit the practice of child brides and child labor are not enforced just like many other laws that grant women equal opportunities and treatment in Kenya.[3]

Few Third World countries have national policies in place to expand access to higher education opportunities for women (Biraimah, 1991), and Kenya is no exception. The education system is a sharp pyramid with girls' enrollments decreasing as they move up the educational ladder. This results in fewer girls than boys in the secondary level and even fewer in the tertiary levels of education (Riria-Ouko, 1984; Economic Survey, 1991; Rathgeber, 1991). Of the 400,000 Kenyan children who complete the primary cycle, only about 40% gain access to secondary schools. In 1990, girls represented 43% of the 171,071 students enrolled in the first year of the secondary level of education (UNICEF/GOK, 1992; Republic of Kenya: Statistical Abstracts, 1991; Republic of Kenya, Women's Bureau/SIDA Project [Swedish International Development Agency] 1993).

Modest progress has been made to increase the number of girls attending the secondary level of education in Kenya. However, the limited number of government-maintained secondary schools for girls, poor course selection, high dropout rates due to exorbitant tuition fees and high pregnancy rates, and curriculum limit girls' education at the secondary level of education (Eshiwani, 1985). In Kenya, girls primarily attend *harambee* schools that have poorer equipment, less-qualified teachers, and more limited curricula than the government-maintained schools that boys are likely to attend (King & Hill, 1993). In 1979, girls represented only 33% of the students in government maintained schools.[4] Several studies have shown that girls' performance in secondary-level examination is better in government-maintained schools than in harambee and better in girls-only schools (King & Hill, 1993).

Government-maintained schools admit students who excel in the national secondary school entrance examinations. Girls, particularly those living in the rural areas, have fewer chances of excelling in these examinations. The rural-urban migration of males to the cities has left women and girls responsible for the domestic labor that sustains a household. The need for girls' labor affects their school attendance and allocation of study time, which in turn affects their school achievement. The majority of the few rural girls who excel in their secondary entrance examinations and who are admitted into government-maintained schools end up in harambee schools because their parents cannot afford to pay tuition, boarding fees, and related fees charged in government-maintained schools. Pressed by lack of resources, most parents are only able to pay the secondary school fees by installments. These arrangements seem only possible in harambee schools where the principal is a member of the same community and knows his or her students' parents.

Girls in the secondary level of education are conditioned to gender-biased learning materials and classroom dynamics that affect their performance in national examinations at all levels of education (Hughes & Mwiria, 1989; Obura, 1992; Osler, 1993). Girls' overall performance in the university entry examinations taken at the end of secondary-level education is poor. This is particularly so in science and mathematics and explains the low representation of girls in science-related careers in tertiary institutions (Eshiwani, 1985). Studies show that girls' performance in science and mathematics is influenced by several factors: the quality of schools that they attend; sexism in schools, particularly in coeducational schools; and anticipated discrimination in the labor market. Girls' performance in science and mathematics has been shown to be better in girls-only schools (Ndunda & Munby, 1991; Rathgeber, 1991). Girls who do not perform well in these subjects are eliminated from the multitude of science-related careers, which are in demand and well remunerated.

Traditional notions of femininity and anticipated discrimination in the labor market limit girls' construction of science futures particularly if they pursue careers that are male-dominated. Girls tend to choose careers that will allow them to eventually prove their femininity by becoming wives and mothers (Ndunda & Munby, 1991).

In 1990, for instance, most girls in the final year of secondary education were enrolled in home economics (87 %) and typing (96.3%), and very few girls chose pure science subjects and/or trades courses in this level. In the same year, girls represented 34% (11,783) of the total number of students enrolled in pure science subjects, and their enrollment in woodwork, metalwork, building construction, power mechanics, and electricity was minimal at 3%, 1%, 8.7%, 4.1%, and 1.9%, respectively (Republic of Kenya, *Statistical Abstracts,* 1991, p. 188).

Therefore, at the primary and secondary levels of education, girls are dropping out of school in considerably large numbers. At the secondary level, they have continued to attend poorer-quality schools in disproportionately high numbers and have restricted access to a broad range of curricula particularly in the sciences. Fewer girls are reaching the tertiary level of education, being encumbered by a plethora of barriers to educational opportunities.

Providing women with more education without changing the gender and power structures that reinforce and perpetuate gender inequities, will not facilitate their access to educational, employment level, and political opportunities equal to those of their male counterparts. The stratification of the society along gender lines makes it possible to limit women's educational opportunities as well as to deny educated, capable women positions of power in a male-dominated sociocultural system (Hughes & Mwiria, 1989). As Feldman (1983) argues, women in Kenya suffer the impact of gender relations, which place them firmly in a position of economic subordination.

Women's Economic Activities

The number of women participating in wage employment in Kenya continues to be low (Economic Survey, 1992). The current employment patterns of women have historical, cultural, social, economic, and political underpinnings. Stamp (1989) argues that central to the nature of African society before colonialism was the prominent role of women in economic production. African women had substantial rights to control the means of production and to own the product of their labor. Women in precolonial Kenya exercised political authority, as sisters of their natal lineage and through their elders' organizations in their marital lineage. With the colonial, postcolonial, and neocolonial eras, women have lost their traditional autonomy and authority (Stamp, 1989; Boserup, 1970).

Robertson and Berger (1986) argue that colonialism introduced urbanization and intensified class and gender differences that existed in precapitalist societies. Cash cropping was introduced mainly to men, who also found more opportunities for wage labor. Pressured by the need to pay taxes, virtually everyone was brought directly or indirectly into the nexus of a commercial economy. Colonialism introduced new mechanisms of exploitation and imposed aspects of Western culture: Christianity, formal education, western technology, higher living standards for the new upper class, and new forms of patriarchal ideology and practice. These have all had a negative impact on the social status of most women in Africa. Colonialism introduced private and public dichotomies in Kenya, as well as mechanisms that drew men into the public space and that limited women's participation within the private sphere.

A study of early wage earners in Kenya by Stichter (1982) shows that opportunities for paid employment were provided by the colonial administrators along gender and racial lines. Men constituted the major source of labor migration but women performed the tasks arising out of the relationship between male wage-earning and the family. The interplay between traditional and the newly emergent division of labor forced women to remain at home, subsidizing the husband's wages through expanded agricultural and trading activities in addition to their household and child-rearing tasks.

The gender-segregated work force that exists today can also be traced to postcolonial policies that regulated entry into the formal employment sector, for example, an examination of postcolonial career-training policies for producing highly skilled African/Kenyan personnel for the modern formal sector reveals the reinforcement of an institutionalized gender segregated work force. In the document entitled "Helping You Choose a Career" produced by the Kenyanization of Personnel Bureau in 1968, a list was given of career opportunities available in government and in the private sector. The prerequisites included sex, age, educational credentials, and subjects in that order. Only two of the 150 careers in the formal employment sector were open to "girls only." These were careers in nursing and in secretarial work. Over half of the career opportunities were open to "boys or men only." The rest were open to both girls and boys and a majority of them required high passing grades in science and mathematics (Republic of Kenya: Ministry of Labour, 1968). Even though the latter careers were "open" to girls, the prerequisites of age and good grades in science and mathematics and the prevailing gender relations eliminated girls from the competition for career training and participation in the formal employment sector.

Although overt gender discrimination policies in the provision of employment opportunities have been replaced with supposedly gender neutral ones, women are still trapped in female preserves of employment. Feldman (1983) argues that in Kenya the prevailing gender relations and the ideology legitimating them continue to prevent women from moving into existing male preserves of employment which, not coincidentally, also command relatively higher wages. This can be associated with women's lack of scientific and technical skills and discrimination against women in the labor market.

The assumption of dependence of women on men has translated into policies that forbid payment of house allowance to women who work for the government and who are married. At present, sex discrimination is not illegal in Kenya, and women find it difficult to challenge laws and policies that discriminate against them. Section 82 of the constitution of Kenya allows discrimination by sex (UNICEF/GOK, 1992).

Current analysis of wage employment by industry and sex shows that female participation as a proportion of total formal/modern[5] sector employment in 1989 was 20.9%, the same level as in 1988. Males accounted for 79.1% of total formal employment and dominated in all industries. Most women are economically active in the informal sector in agriculture, crafts, or commerce as low-level, self-employed producers or traders. They are rarely in the new economic sectors considered vital for future economic development such as manufacturing, science, technology, and communications.

In all of the occupations, women earn significantly less than their male counterparts. Comparisons of men and women's earnings in regular employment conceal the fact that "over a fifth of women employed in the formal sector are employed as casuals, and hence in worse conditions with worse terms of service than regular employees" (ILO, Jobs and Skills Programme for Africa [JASPA], 1981, pp. 5–6). Women's total average earnings amount to less than half (49%) of men's. In 1988, 92.6% of most senior civil servants were men who earned the highest salaries in the civil service scale. Women constituted 25% of all civil servants in 1988 and 92% of them were in Job Group G (salary level) and below, the higher rank being Group T and the lowest being Group A. Only 8.2 % of females were on or above Job Group H, the starting scale for most university graduates[6] (Republic of Kenya, Women's Bureau/SIDA Project, 1992, p. 12).

Women living in the rural areas are multiply disadvantaged when it comes to wage employment. They have less formal education making it difficult for them to compete in the formal employment sector. The rural-urban development dichotomy, with an emphasis on an urban-based formal employment sector, has made it difficult for women to participate in wage employment. The concentration of both the formal and informal employment sectors in the urban areas has left rural areas with minimum employment opportunities. Because of the unavailability of employment and the demanding gender specific roles that occupy women's daily lives, their employment participation rates in the rural areas are less than in the urban areas (JASPA, 1981). The dichotomy between "man the producer" and "woman the reproducer" is accentuated, though in reality rural women assume functions well beyond the role usually associated with a "housewife." In rural areas in most parts of Africa, women do 30% of ploughing, 50% of planting, 60% of livestock work, 60% of harvesting, 70% of weeding, 85% of processing and storing, and 95% of domestic work (Chlebowska, 1990).

Women's tasks have increased in difficulty and intensity with the migration of men to the cities in search of employment; increased primary education of children, particularly girls; and population pressure that has resulted in more intensive land use. Although women bear all the domestic responsibilities, they are often forced to carry out extra work such as traditional beer brewing[7] or hiring themselves out as casual laborers on neighboring farms in order to meet household financial needs (JASPA, 1981). Rural women in Kenya are burdened by heavy work loads, which impede their participation in economic activities.

It is important to note that very few rural women have found employment in these plantations and farms because these employment opportunities are limited to a few geographical regions. Only 17% of Kenya is arable land, and Kilome division, which is the region of Kenya where I collected data for this book lies outside these regions. There are no farms and plantations in Kilome division and/or in the neighboring divisions in which women can find wage employment. Kilome women have stringent, more limited income opportunities than those women in regions where there are big farms, plantations, or factories. Thus, women's conditions are structured by complex situations that have similarities as well as differences. Just as women are not a monolith, rural women cannot be assumed to be subject to similar situations irrespective of their age, marital status, and setting.

With the limited employment opportunities for women, particularly for those who constitute almost 80% of the rural population, land becomes an invaluable resource. Women who have access to arable land are able to generate income from small-hold farming. Their independent access to land is crucial. Without land, they cannot plant food to feed their families. In addition, they cannot acquire credit, since land is the only property that rural people can use as collateral. Women's farm income, particularly in female-headed households is limited by the size of accessible holding and by access to labor and farm machinery. Women who live with their husbands face the problem of overall farm resources and of the distribution of income realized through crop sales. Although women contribute almost all the labor toward cultivation, they do not have an automatic right to the use of the income from the sale of cash crops. I can remember vividly my mother's punishment for withdrawing money from the coffee account even though she provided all the labor. She picked the coffee, took it to the factory on her back-a five-mile (8 kilometers) distance carrying over fifty kilograms of coffee.

The need for women to feed, clothe, and educate their children stipulates that they work as casual laborers or cultivate food crops and vegetables, which they sell to their neighbors and in local markets. These needs have increased their work load.

Women and the Family

Studies of African families in precolonial times allude to a gender-based sharp division of labor in the family (Muthiani, 1973). Most of the ethnic groups in Kenya practiced bridewealth marriage system. Through marriage, women were (and still are) affiliated to their husband's patrilineage and secured lineage membership for their offspring. Hakansson (1988) argues that among the Abagusii, a wife was under the complete formal authority of her husband and no party outside the homestead could interfere with their relationship. Stamp (1989) disputes the idea of an autonomous male head of household in bridewealth systems. She argues that in the complexity of the family in precolonial Africa, authority and power were not conterminous. "Relationships between fathers and sons, between brothers, between co-wives and their husband, and between sisters and brothers made it very difficult to assign 'head of household' status to one individual" (p. 56).

In the modern setting, the image of a woman as a potential mother and wife remains. McAdoo and Were (1987) argue that family life is very important for women and men in Kenya. Women still play important roles in family networks. The family, and in particular motherhood, offers a woman the opportunity to exert her influence as both elder sister and mother of grown sons living in the same household. This implies that the concept of a family in the African context is complex. It is not a bounded unit of society that consists of a man and his family (Stamp, 1989). In Kenya, motherhood is a powerful conceptual weapon used by both progressive and conservative forces in the battle to define women's political and social place (Stamp, 1995). Single motherhood, however, is not considered honorable.

Regardless of what benefits motherhood accrues to women, in the present setting women continue to bear the main responsibility for the welfare of families and must provide the physical labor required to accomplish these domestic tasks. In the present social, economic, and political circumstances in Kenya, the responsibilities of women, and mothers and wives in particular, have increased tremendously. In colonial and postcolonial times, the sexual division of labor along gender lines has become a relationship of dominance and exploitation of women in their provision of nonwage labor (Freeman, 1988).

Kenyan women's experiences of labor both in the private and public sphere are not uniform, for instance, the domestic tasks of urban, middle-class, educated, waged Kenyan women could not be similar to those of peasant women living in the rural areas or in the urban slums of Nairobi. Women's experiences are structured by class, culture, religion, and other ideological institutions and frameworks (Mohanty, 1991).

Stichter and Parpart's (1988) study on middle-class families in Nairobi found that the wife is by far the principal person responsible for domestic work.

A working wife and mother is also responsible for finding a house girl to help out with domestic work. This means that if the house girl leaves, which is often the case, the woman has to arrange for alternate childcare until she finds a replacement. Consequently, like most mothers in developing countries, mothers in Kenya face tremendous pressure to balance their careers and the traditional homemaker roles. In most cases, this becomes impossible because of the separation between the home and the workplace.

The work space is not organized to take into account the women's numerous responsibilities as wives, mothers, workers, and all the other responsibilities that women undertake as members of extended families. The separation between the public and private spheres limits women's participation in wage employment. It also gives employers the leeway to discriminate and to exploit women as workers. Women are denied positions of power on claims that their gender roles as mothers and wives make them unsuitable for such positions. In the present setting, elements of patrilineal sexual division of labor from precapitalist societies have been retained in dominated and distorted forms and combined with Victorian and Christian notions of male superiority to create an image of women that reflects inferiority (Obbo, 1980; Stamp, 1989).

In the household, an employed wife is faced with contradictions as she is viewed with ambivalence (Munachonga, 1988). On one side, her income is perceived as having financial advantages for her husband because it relieves his economic burdens and enables him to keep more of his earnings for personal use or on other wives he may have, since polygymy is sanctioned under customary law. At the same time, the wife's access to independent income has a negative effect on marriage and family stability (Munachonga, 1988). For many women, maintaining a balance between a successful career and making a home is a stressful exercise. As Kiiti (1993) observes, it is like swimming against the current.

For women in the rural areas, their nonwaged activities are almost limitless. They perform the bulk of work required to sustain the household that includes subsistence agriculture, childrearing, care for the aged and sick, and housework. Women's reproductive and productive roles have been intensified with male migration from the rural areas. This phenomenon has resulted in de facto female heads of households where husbands are away for long periods of time leaving the wife to support the family, although the husband's income may be supplied on an irregular basis (Due, 1991).

Rural women are the backbone of Kenyan peasantry and are doubly dominated as peasants who are a dominated class within underdeveloped capitalism, and as women who are a dominated category within the peasantry. Rural women's labor is exploited to maintain the unequal exchange of primary commodities on the international markets (Stamp, 1986, 1989). Wages in underdeveloped countries are rarely sufficient to support a family; therefore, women are expected to engage in subsistence agriculture for the survival of the family. The provision of nonwaged labor by women and the growing of food for subsistence and sale on marginal land, is necessary for the continuation of the unequal exchange upon which the sale of primary commodities on the world market is based (Freeman, 1988).

An examination of women's individual and group activities in Kenya reveals their concerted efforts to retain control of their work. In Kenya, women's resistance[8] to the appropriation of their labor by men and by the state has taken many forms, including refusal to adopt new cultivation practices, refusal to grow certain crops, or cutting back on their production. Stamp (1989) points out that the channeling of women's earnings into self-help groups is a form of their resistance to the appropriation of their labor by the international commodity market through the agency of their husbands or male relatives.

Women's Self-Help Groups

Women in rural communities are using precolonial gender-based organizing strategies to form women's self-help groups to cope, shape, and resist their social conditions characterized by harsh economic, social, and political changes. These groups in the traditional setting became necessary as a collective geared at identifying a task and at putting their resources together to work on the task (Republic of Kenya: Women's Bureau/SIDA Project, 1992). Women's customary organizations, such as age-groups for the Kikuyu, Myethya, or working parties for the Kamba, have developed into self-help groups with new functions overlaying the old (Stamp, 1986). The original objectives of the traditional organizations have changed to accommodate the rapid political and socioeconomic changes taking place in the country.

Women's self-help groups have grown to be associated with the harambee or community self-help movement whose main objective is mobilizing and revitalizing Kenyans in the development process of the country. The Ministry of Social Services defines a women's group as a voluntary self-help group of more than fifteen members made up exclusively of women. The ministry adds that in those groups that have men as members, it is the women who have to exercise decision making powers (Republic of Kenya: Women's Bureau/SIDA Project, 1992). The underlying reason for women's self-help groups' formation and existence is the increasing burden assumed by women in the changing social division of labor. These groups have risen as an instrument through which the individual member can strengthen her capabilities in meeting the challenges of being the chief provider for her family's welfare.

Women's self-help groups have emerged throughout much of the rural areas as a response to economic, social, political, and technological changes arising from the colonial experience, from participation in a cash economy, and from policies and politics of independent Kenya (Thomas, 1985). These groups are involved in their own income-generating activities, such as producing handicrafts for sale, or assisting in building community facilities. Typical activities of women's self-help groups include farming, milling maize, keeping livestock, making handicrafts, and maintaining rental properties. They also operate revolving loan schemes or credit. They extend credit to women who are associated with these groups and who are pursuing small-scale enterprises (UNICEF/GOK, 1992). They also provide loans to women for education and medical expenses.

Women's self-help groups must register with the Women's Bureau, Ministry of Social Services that was set up in 1975, the International Women's Year. This is a political move to control opposition to the government, thus limiting women's social and political power. The Women's Bureau has become both the effective focus for policies toward women and a major means of acquiring international funds for aid specifically directed toward women (Feldman, 1983).

In her study that focused on women's self-help groups in the rural community of Murang'a, Kenya, Ahlberg-Maina (1991) argues that these groups in rural Kenya are still an important resource for change. She posits that in the context of Kenyan history, women have continued to exploit the power of collective action to counteract negative forces within the system even after colonial forces had disrupted their culture and collective organization.

> Continued collective participation of women has not just offered a link between the past and the present, it constitutes a process of consciously selecting positive cultural traits and adapting them to meet new challenges. It is perhaps only through such dynamic participation that issues, which evoke resistance, can become an integral part of the collective activity and social order. (P. 187)

Stamp (1986) argues that women's self-help groups are not simply about cooperative development projects, or strategies for coping with change; rather, they are vital organizations for resistance to exploitation. She argues that by women channeling the cash from crops into these organizations, they are preventing appropriation of their product by their husbands. Their attempt to "accumulate capital is a means of protecting and enhancing their fragile incomes and compensating for lost domestic production" (Stamp, 1986, p. 40). Consequently, women have become agents of resistance and change in the maelstrom of contemporary Kenyan affairs. Their agency resides in their communal endeavors and is constantly reinvented in the context of political and social changes (Stamp, 1995).

Conclusion

This examination of Kenyan women's participation in education, the economy, the family, and in the general society shows that their experiences are structured by gender and power relations that limit their access to equal opportunities. These relations are related to the historical, cultural, economic, and political legacies of society. The colonial economy that was imposed on indigenous Kenyans dismantled cultural values and customs, which supported African social systems. Colonial administrators, who were invariably men, brought their assumptions of male supremacy with them. They did not seek spokeswomen or head women, but spokesmen and headmen. When the need for semiskilled workers developed, young boys were sought for schooling. The political power of women was not recognized by Westerners because it was always indirect, often a function of their position as sisters, wives, or mothers. Under the increasingly stringent and competitive circumstances of postcolonial capitalism, patrilineages are becoming more patriarchal, intensifying control over lineage wives and undermining the power and rights to resources of lineage sisters (Stamp, 1991; Boserup, 1970). Precapitalist dominant gender relations have been manipulated to exploit and to dominate women and to deny them social, economic, and political power in present-day Kenya.

Present patterns of women's participation in education and formal employment show that these institutions are still gender-segregated. Parity in enrollments of girls and boys at the primary level are accompanied by high dropout rates of girls due to pregnancy, child marriages, and high fees charged as a result of the implementation of cost-sharing strategies. Girls have limited access to secondary-level education and they continue to attend schools of poor quality in disproportionately high numbers. They also have restricted access to a broad range of curricula, particularly in the sciences. They are conditioned to biased-learning materials and classroom dynamics.

Women represent about 22% of the total formal wage employment. The demand for educational credentials, discrimination against women, and maintenance of a sharp division of labor in the family continues to keep women out of more generally lucrative careers and out of the formal employment sector. Women living in the rural areas have less employment opportunities than their urban and educated female counterparts.

Rural women, who do not have educational credentials and resources such as access to land, are seriously disadvantaged. The rural-urban dichotomy severely limits their opportunities for employment. The women's participation in income-generating opportunities is limited by the conglomerate of labor intensive nonwaged activities that they engage in for their family's survival.

Women have become intervention agents and buffers for their families from the effects of the social, economic, and political crises that have befallen Africa with little or no support from their governments. The government of Kenya has consistently maintained the position that women are not discriminated against and therefore do not need to struggle for rights, for they are already enjoying them. Sweeping and vaguely worded statements of government commitment and intentions about women in development are expressed in national development plans and in party manifestos (Nzomo, 1989). As Staudt and Glickman (1989) observe, the Nairobi meeting to conclude "the United Nations Decade for Women in 1985 signalled no dramatic changes in African governments' responsiveness to women or in women's voice in the political process" (p. 4). Women in Kenya continue to be encumbered by a plethora of gender barriers to educational, economic, and political opportunities. Such barriers make gender and power crucial categories of analysis in any attempt to understand and to address gender inequities in Kenya.

3

Research Sites

The research is set in Kilome division because of my own interests and relationship with the area. Also, this region is a part of rural Kenya that illustrates the difficulties that rural women face in their attempt to participate in the educational, economic, social, and political spheres of the society. Their experiences are issues that are of interest to me not only as an educator, but also as a woman who was born and schooled in Kilome.

My fieldwork took place in the Kithumba and Kyandue villages and in Salama, a small town along the Nairobi-Mombasa highway in Kilome division, Makueni District. Makueni District is in the Eastern Province of the Republic of Kenya and is one of the six districts of this province. Makueni District is divided into three divisions, namely, Kilome, Kibwezi, and Makueni. Women in Kilome division belong to the Akamba ethnic group. A member of the Akamba ethnic group is called a Muûkamba, many are Akamba or Kamba, the language is Kiikamba, and the region is Ukamba (Muthiani, 1973). (See map 3.1.)

Kilome division lies about 130 kilometers south of Nairobi, the capital of Kenya. In 1990, Kilome division had a population density of 275 persons/kilometer^2 or a total of approximately 241,900 people (Ondiege, 1992). It borders Kajiando division to the west, Makueni to the east, Kibwezi to the south, and Mbooni to the north. Kilome town is the divisional headquarters with a population of about 1,500[1] at present. The headquarters is a subsidiary of the office of the president and it houses the offices of the district officer, divisional social development assistant, and a police station. The district officer is a presidential appointee. Kilome division is divided into locations and sublocations that consist of several villages headed by a chief

25

26

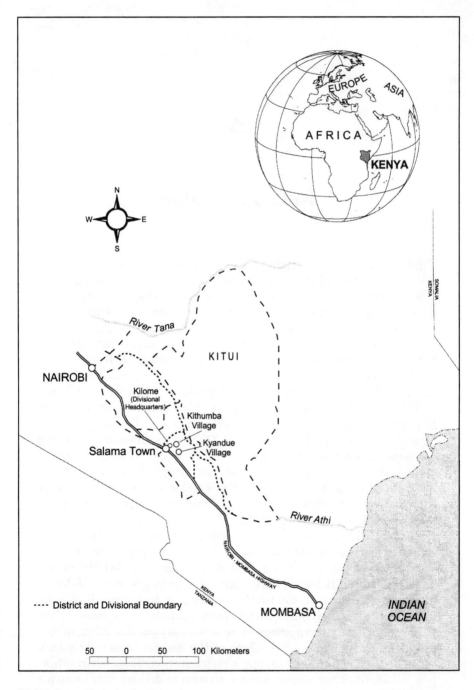

MAP 3.1 Research Sites

and assistant chiefs. Since their creation during the colonial era, these positions have been held by men who are appointed by the Public Service Commission, the body in charge of hiring civil servants.

Kithumba Village

Kithumba village is in Kilome division, Makueni District. It covers an area of about twelve square kilometers and has a population of about 4,200 people. Kithumba is on the Kilome-Salama road, up the hills about 2.5 kilometers from Kilome divisional headquarters where the offices of the district officer (DO) and other administrative offices are located. The Kilome-Salama road, which passes through Kithumba, is tarmacked. There is also a power-line that runs from Salama through Kithumba to Precious Blood Girls' School, the only government-maintained girls' secondary school in this division. This power-line was constructed after the president of Kenya visited the school and was impressed by the school's academic excellence. In the prevailing political climate in Kenya, the president's act was construed as a favor to his political stalwart, a senior civil servant whose home is a few kilometers to the south of this school, located about twelve kilometers northwest of Kithumba village. An additional favor to tarmac the road from Nunguni to this Precious Blood Girls School stalled, and was eventually abandoned, when this civil servant retired.

Life in Kithumba Village

Each family in Kithumba village owns a small plot ranging in size between one and four acres. Here maize and beans are planted during the rainy seasons. Rainfall in the area is inadequate and unpredictable, a factor that when combined with shallow soils, steep slopes, and unstable surface soil structures, makes water and soil conservation a delicate issue. Consequently, harvests are poor and most families buy Akamba diet food—mainly maize and beans *(isyo)*—throughout the year.

Women from Kithumba earn their income from small-scale agriculture, petty trading, casual (temporary) work, and participation in women's self-help groups. There are no big farms or plantations where they may find paid employment. Women utilize their plots efficiently and in most cases overuse their plots in their attempt to increase productivity. In a family's plot, one can find sections for subsistence crops, vegetables, poultry, and livestock (usually one cow and two goats). A few families have planted coffee,[2] the only cash crop planted in this area. Some women in Kithumba village are petty traders. They sell vegetables, chickens, and eggs, and those who have cows sell milk to their neighbors. Some take their commodities to the local market that assembles on a weekly basis. Others take their commodities to several other markets within the division. A woman's mobility depends on the age of her children, availability of help when she is away and, more importantly, permission from her husband.

There is one hospital and two health centers accessible to the people of Kithumba village. Although these centers are not within walking distances, there is adequate means of transport. The hospital, which has a visiting qualified doctor, is run by the Precious Blood Catholic sisters. One health center is run by a local church, and the other by the government. The latter is supposed to offer free medical services to the local people. However, with the current government cuts on spending on health and social services, this center is understaffed and lacks basic drugs.

Schooling in Kithumba

There is no school inside the village but Kilome nursery, primary, and harambee secondary schools lie just outside the village. The children of this village go to these various schools located between three and six kilometers from the village. Some children, particularly those in secondary schools have to walk long distances to their schools. None of the girls from this village was attending Precious Blood Girls School at the time of my study.

Kilome's secondary school was built by the community in 1979. As a harambee school, it receives minimum assistance from the government. Most teachers who are posted from the universities by the government to teach at this school never report. They always try to be reposted to other areas.

Kithumba Women's Self-Help Group

I went to Kithumba village because I grew up here. My first meeting was attended by about fifty women. The discussions I had with these women, particularly those from Kyandue, encouraged Kithumba women to form a women's group in their village, since no women's self-help group existed.

A few women from Kithumba were members of other women's self-help groups in neighboring villages. These included the Uvuuni

Welfare Organization, which has male membership, and Kwa Muulu, which is associated with the GreenBelt movement. This movement encourages environmental awareness and makes tree-planting an income-generating activity for women. The women felt that since every home has a baby girl, it was extremely important to make sure that these girls did not leave school prematurely as their mothers did. Since they noted that education provided a sure escape from poverty they decided to form a new women's self-help group in which they would include education of girls as a major goal. The women agreed that each member should pay 100 Kenya shillings ($2) to become a full member. This money was to be paid over a period of not more than ten months. In addition to the membership fee, each member had to pay a 10 Kenya shillings as a registration fee. The women agreed that they would be meeting fortnightly. I became a member of this group and attended six meetings.

Kyandue Village

Kyandue village is also in Kilome division, Makueni District. It lies eight kilometers east of Kithumba and south of the divisional headquarters at Kilome. Kyandue is surrounded by very high hills, which isolate this village from other centers particularly in the rainy season. It occupies an area of about fifteen square kilometers and has a population of about 6,500.

Life in Kyandue Village

Each family in Kyandue village has a piece of land where members grow subsistence crops, mainly maize, beans, and pigeon peas in the rainy season. Some of the plots that range from 2.5 to 5 acres yield high harvests, while others have poor harvests. Kyandue is warmer than Kithumba; this accelerates the maturity of food crops and so, yields are much higher in Kyandue than in Kithumba. Most of the families own some livestock, the number depending on the size of the family's plot. Those with bigger plots keep cows and goats; those with smaller plots keep a few goats that are often tethered. A good number of families practice zero grazing wherein the livestock are fed and given water in the barn; women are responsible for this chore.

Women in Kyandue village earn income from selling vegetables, onions, bananas, milk, and excess farm produce (maize and beans; working as casual laborers; and participating in women's self-help groups' income-generating activities. A few women grow coffee in their plots. Coffee, the only cash crop planted in this area, belongs to the man as the head of the household. Women have no control over the income from it, although they are responsible for cultivating, picking, transporting, and cleaning the berries at the coffee factory. They do not count on income from coffee sales.

Kyandue village has no health center. The nearest one is about ten kilometers away and there is no means of transport to this center. In addition, the center, like all other government health centers, only handles simple ailments. Serious cases are dealt with at Kikoko hospital, fifteen kilometers away, or at Machakos general hospital, ninety kilometers away. Most people prefer to go to Kikoko hospital, which is run by the Precious Blood Catholic Sisters. This is a private hospital, but fees are subsidized by the Catholic mission.

The major difficulty that the people of Kyandue face is transportation. Kyandue village almost resembles a cone with hilly slopes. One major road runs on its circumference. On one arc, the road is all weather; on the other arc, it is seasonal. There are no major roads running within the village. During the rainy seasons, the seasonal roads are so impassable that families have had to carry their dead in a casket over a distance of three kilometers down the slopes to the village for burial.

Schooling in Kyandue

Kyandue village has a few nursery and primary schools but no harambee secondary school; the nearest one is in the neighboring village about six kilometers away on the hills. It receives little support from the government; therefore, all the teachers in this school are grade 12 graduates who hold advanced level certificates. In some cases, Bachelor of Arts graduates who fail to find employment in the city offer their services in these schools. Most teachers are temporary, and that affects the students' performance in the national examinations. Few students from harambee schools here or elsewhere in the region go to the university. Very few students from Kyandue village qualify to go to Precious Blood Girls Secondary School, which is about fifteen kilometers away.

Kyandue Women's Self-Help Group

Kyandue village has one major women's self-help group that is divided into sections A and B. The women noted that there are certain times when it is convenient and necessary to operate as one group, particularly when doing community work such as building gabions[3] for soil conservation, and other times when they see it necessary to work as separate groups.

Membership in one section of the group is limited to women married to men from the Ambua clan.[4] This group formalizes marriages of women married to Ambua men by paying bridewealth. The Ambua women's subgroup of the Kyandue women's self-help group was formed out of a crisis when a woman married to a Mumbua man died, and a dispute arose over whether the husband could claim her body and children since he had not paid the bridewealth. Other women married in this clan, who traditionally are taken as cowives, felt that their counterpart was mistreated in death and vowed that they would not permit a repeat of that incident. The widower had to pay bridewealth to his deceased wife's parents so that he could bury her and keep the children they had had together.

The Ambua women's self-help group meets once a week. They bring firewood to one member each week and contribute 10 Kenya shillings ($0.25). The money is kept by the treasurer, and it is used to buy goats and other gifts that are presented to a bride's parents as bridewealth before marriage. Similarly, the women present gifts to parents of women whose marriages were not formalized. This is in line with Akamba traditions; however, there is no fixed amount that the women have to pay.

The combined group, which has forty members, meets twice a month. The ages vary between twenty and sixty years. They pay 10 Kenya shillings ($0.25) during each meeting. The women also plant bananas for their members. Each meeting is held at the plot of a member who must have previously prepared eighty holes to plant the bananas. The women use some of the money they contribute to buy bar soap and kerosene; which are kept at members' homes and is accessible to all members who are expected to buy their own commodities instead of going to the shops. The profit goes to the women's joint account. They also give loans to members and non-members at differential interest rates.

Salama Town

Salama is a unique town in Kilome division. It is about 125 kilometers south of Nairobi and about ten kilometers from Kithumba and Kyandue villages on the Nairobi-Mombasa highway. This highway is part of the trans-African highway. Salama has a population of about 1,000. The people come from villages around Salama and from other regions of the country.

Life in Salama

Salama is a town that attracts girls from the villages who use Salama as a gateway to the city and to larger towns. Business in Salama is geared toward providing service to the truckers and also to the local community. The truckers ply between Rwanda, Uganda, Sudan, and the port of Mombasa. A good number of the girls work as barmaids in the beer halls, and others work in the hotels. The middle-aged women, some of whom were once barmaids, run some of the hotel and bar businesses, and others are petty traders who sell vegetables, potatoes, tomatoes, and onions. Others sell *miraa*—"leafy antisleeping stems" that are chewed by truck drivers, especially the Somali. A few of the women are seamstresses.

Salama does not have a good image because of the truckers. The Nairobi-Mombasa highway is considered to be part of the AIDS corridor of Africa. Salama town is associated with "immorality," and women who live and work there are assumed to be promiscuous. Women compose a good proportion of Salama's population.

There is no hospital in Salama; there is, however, a private clinic that provides emergency services. The nearest health center is about twenty kilometers away, and major hospitals can be found in Nairobi and in Machakos. The roads linking Salama to major centers in the country are tarmacked. However, roads linking Salama to the interior have no regular public service vehicles.

Schooling in Salama

The only school in Salama town is a Madrassa, an Islamic religious school at the mosque. The nearest nursery and primary schools are about 1.5 kilometers from Salama along the highway and there is a harambee secondary school about 5 kilometers away. None of the girls in Salama go to Precious Blood Girls School.

Salama Women's Self-Help Group

Up till the time I went to Salama there was no women's group. People living in Salama did not seem to have a strong sense of community as those in the villages. However, the women who participated in this study expressed the need to form a women's group so that they could continue meeting when the study was over. They agreed to welcome three men into their group. The Women's Bureau in the Ministry of Social Services allows a few men to join women's groups on the condition that they don't take leadership roles. However, male patronage in these groups has became an issue of concern. Urdvardy (1988) points out that the patron-client relationship found between women's self-help groups and certain males affects the independence and success of these groups' projects.

The first meeting was attended by seven women and one man. Each member was asked to pay a membership fee of 140 Kenya shillings ($2.75) within a week. The membership fee was used to build a shelter and to buy eggs and soft drinks for resale. The progress the group was making attracted more women than the group could admit. The women limited membership in the women's group to eighteen. The women agreed that there was a need to come together and to begin to address issues that affect them as individuals and as a group. The women identified poverty as a major impediment to their education and to that of their children. The group's goal was to save money to purchase a maize mill, which would increase their income and enable them to afford to give their children meaningful educational opportunities.

During my work with the women's group in Salama, it became evident that women living in the town had differences among themselves that limited their interactions. These included type of business and employment, marital status, and age. Women who operated their own or family businesses and who were married were more comfortable with each other. Single older businesswomen, most of them who had previously worked as barmaids, also tended to relate together more favorably. And, younger women, who were currently working as barmaids related better with women who had previously worked as barmaids. These kinds of groupings seem to have some relation to images that the women of Salama want to portray. It seemed to me that those married businesswomen want to show the world that their business is "clean." This could be a struggle to shape a different image for Salama, which is perceived by people, particularly those living in the villages in the interior, as an immoral town.

The major difference between life in the villages and that in Salama, a transrural town, is the "atomistic" life-style that people in Salama seem to lead. One participant pointed out rather regretfully that "people in Salama live as entities, and no one cares about what the other does. Each one here does whatever he or she desires. You concentrate on your business, if that is what you do. If it succeeds, it does; if it doesn't, that's it for you. If you need help, maybe your friends will give some help. Otherwise, we do not live the way people live in the villages" (Interview, July 1994).

Choice of Study Area

I entered Kilome division, the site of my research, partly as an insider and as an outsider. I am a Muûkamba, born in Uvuuni, a village in Kilome, the child of Jonah Kiluva and Hannah Ndoti. I attended a local primary school and left the village school in 1973 to undertake my secondary-level education in a city secondary school. I sat for the Kenya Primary Certificate of Education examinations in 1972, and was admitted to an harambee day school about ten kilometers from my home and lived with relatives whose rural home was nearer to the school. My educational prospects would have been better if I had been admitted to one of the government secondary schools in the country or attended Precious Blood, the only government girls-only school in Kilome. Precious Blood Girls Secondary School takes only six girls from the three divisions of Makueni District, making the school very competitive.

The harambee school I attended, like most schools of this genre, was very inferior. There were no trained teachers, no facilities or equipment required to teach science, and no vocational subjects that had been made compulsory. I stayed in this school for two months. Had it not been for my brother's intervention (who had graduated from high school and was working as a trainee accountant), I would certainly have failed my university entry examination if I had not dropped out of school before sitting for this examination. My brother found a space for me in Kenya High School, a former European girls' high school that charged higher fees. He paid my school fees for the six years I was a student in the school. School fees were a barrier to many girls, particularly, rural girls.

My experiences of education in the village primary school and in the high-cost high school were extremely different. In my primary school, which was coeducational, the teachers, mostly male, in the upper primary level treated girls and boys differently. They intimidated, harassed, and embarrassed girls, particularly those who were mature. The classroom environment was always very tense and hostile. There was a tendency to portray girls as dumb. The treatment most girls received eroded their self-confidence and self-esteem. The teaching methods were very traditional, and teachers were autocratic and authoritarian. I do not remember any girl asking a question in the class! If you didn't understand when the teacher was teaching, you were doomed unless you had older siblings or relatives whom you could consult after school. Most of the girls in my class were the only ones in the school and had gone that far with formal education in their families. It is not surprising that most of these girls left school at the primary level and got married. The shift from the rural life to an urban elite school, Kenya High School, was a major challenge for me. The world represented in this school was totally different from that I had known. I had grown up in the rural area, and most of the children in this urban school had grown up in the city, most of whom came from homes with a very different socioeconomic status from mine. Their background was reflected in their dress, language, attitudes, and experiences that transversed nations. I was a village girl who had grown up in a polygamous home collecting firewood and water, digging, planting, and harvesting. My classmates had middle-class mothers as their role models, whereas my role models were completely different. It was a struggle to fit in this school. Nevertheless, once I reconciled the two "worlds," I began to tap the benefits of this environment. The teachers had high expectations of the students, and girls aspired for higher education and challenging careers in science, science-related fields, and in the arts.

I wanted to become a medical doctor; therefore, I chose science and mathematics subjects for my advanced level education (grade 12 and 13 equivalent). After completing this level of education I was called to the university to pursue a B.Ed. (science) degree.

I went to Kilome division, taking with me my two children aged eight and nine, to talk to some of the women about their educational experiences of education. I wanted the women to share with me their stories of formal education, highlighting the barriers that they faced and those that their children, and in particular their daughters face. I also wanted to find out how they were constructing educational possibilities for their children and girls in particular. This is why I made my journey to Kithumba and Kyandue villages and to Salama town in Kilome Division to talk to women who had not been as "fortunate" as I had been. My journey from Kilome to Kenya High School to Canada and back to Kilome would not have been possible without my brother's intervention.

My participation in the study and my "double identity" as a native of Kilome and as a woman-scholar committed to women's liberation and justice influenced the women's conceptualization of their subordination and agency. The discussions that I held with the women as individuals and as a group provided the opportunity for the women to examine their compliance and to figure out ways to challenge patriarchy. I found myself asking the women to move beyond "sacrificing" themselves to create solutions, but to also to begin to question and challenge the structures that perpetuate women's exploitation and subordination. I used my "double consciousness" of privilege and subordination, as an educated woman and as a Kenyan woman, as a methodological and political opportunity to challenge the women to question the structures that maintain their subordination (Mies, 1983).

This background shaped my choice of site, and indeed influenced my discussions with the women of Kilome division. The discussions highlighted the women's experiences, making visible the constraints that they face and their active participation in shaping their social conditions and those of their children.

Participants

While in Kilome division, I held several meetings in the villages and in Salama town. These meetings were attended by a total of about one hundred and twenty women. As summarized in table 3.1 on participants, thirty women from the villages and transrural town of Salama volunteered to talk with me about their experiences of education, that of their children, and about their day-to-day experiences. In addition, three professional women, born and partly schooled in Kilome but now living in Nairobi, and five high school girls in Kithumba and Kyandue villages agreed to participate in this study. The high school girls' mothers were among the women in the villages who participated in the study.

The ages of the rural women and of those living in Salama ranged from nineteen to seventy-five years. Their level of education ranged from 0 to 18+. As Ahlberg-Maina (1991) notes, older women continue to hold positions of power in the women's self-help groups, even though they might be illiterate. The older women's experiences are important because their views give a picture of how cultural assumptions about women's roles have changed over a relatively short period of time.

The ages of the three professional women ranged between thirty-five and thirty-eight years. The professional women are the role models rural women would like their daughters to emulate. Some rural women idealize education as a panacea to the social and economic difficulties that women face. However, the professional women's stories attest to the fact that women's educational and economic inequities do not disappear with a good education.

TABLE 3.1 Participants: A Summary

Name[1]	Years of formal education	Village	Age	Number of children	Married	Separated	Widowed	Single
Mwelu	4	Kithumba	40	7	✔			
Mumo	4	Kithumba	75	7	✔			
Mulee	7	Kithumba	44	8	✔			
Mwikali	3	"	54	7	✔			
Catherine	7	"	37	5	✔			
Kanini	4	"	46	7			✔	
Maria	13	"	30	3		✔		
Rose	9	Kithumba	36	10	✔			
Wayua	0	"	46	8			✔	
Mutinda	7	Kithumba	30	5		✔		
Teresia	1	Kithumba	50	10	✔			
Wanza	7	Kithumba	34	7	✔			
Janet	9	Kyandue	33	5	✔			
Ruth	7	Kyandue	45	7	✔			
Ndunge	7	"		7	✔			
Ndele	6	Kyandue	36	5	✔			
Ngina	3	Kyandue	42	8	✔			
Rachel	7	Kyandue	39	5	✔			
Meli	1	Kyandue	45	7			✔	
Faith[2]	11	Kyandue[2]	32	5	✔[2]			
Katunge	11	"	36	3	✔			
Nzula	9	Kyandue	38	4	✔			
Mariya	7	Kyandue	42	10	✔			
Kavuli	7	Kyandue	28	4	✔			
Kasika	0	Kyandue	38	8			✔	
Kadogo	7	Kyandue	33	3				✔
Nzeli	4	Kyandue	70	7	✔			
Beth	9	Salama		8	✔			
Mbeti	7	Salama	35	0				✔
Kamene	3	Salama	37	4				✔
Wanza	3	Salama	33	1				✔
Kambua	8	Salama	19	0				✔
Nduki	7	Salama	35	2				✔
Wausi (P)	18+		35	1				✔
Mutheu (P)	17		38	3	✔			
Koki (P)	16		35	1				✔
Ndinda (S)	11		17	0				✔
Jane (S)	12		17	0				✔
Munee (S)	12		18	0				✔
Waeni (S)	12		18	0				✔
Mueni (S)	9		15	0				✔

1. I have used pseudonyms.

2. The latest information I have from Kithumba and Kyandue women is that Faith has moved back to her father's house leaving her five children behind. She is a member of a women's group that gives assistance to children of "runaway" mothers.

P = Professional

S = Student

4

Grounding the Methodology of Study

This chapter discusses the methodology of the study on which this book is based. The study explored Kilome women's experiences of educational policies. Like many other women, Kilome women's voices and concerns have been excluded in the official discourse on education and development articulated in policy documents. This exclusion has led to the formulation not only of gender-biased policies but also of seemingly gender neutral policies that have served to exacerbate gender inequalities in Kenya.

Aware of the problematics of speaking for and about others, I strove[1] to provide the rural women with the opportunity to narrate their experiences of education from their own standpoints. I encouraged them to articulate their thoughts, fears, and hopes on the subjects of education, paid and unpaid work, family, and sexuality. Even though I understood the issues that women in my village faced, I was conscious of how formal, Western higher education had privileged and distanced me from the reality of these women. The complexity of colonialism and schooling in formal institutions (both in Africa and in the Western world) produce academics who are alienated from their communities and who are capable of producing racist, classist, and sexist research irrespective of their own race, gender, and class.

In this chapter, the discussion on theory guiding how the research should proceed is followed by an examination of issues around writing ethnography. Lastly, I reflect on doing research as both an insider and outsider in Kilome division.

Paving the Way: Theoretical Framework

Distinctions between supposed public and private spheres of human existence have generated a lot of controversy. Jaggar (1983) points out that traditional political theory has always made a distinction between the public and the private spheres of human existence. She notes that political theorists, though unable to agree on where the line between public and private spheres should be drawn, have unanimously agreed that the areas of sexuality, childbearing, and childrearing should be defined as the private sphere because these activities have been conceived as natural or biologically determined. Jaggar concludes that:

> When so much of the work in the "private" realm is invariably done by women, moreover, it is not just irrational but sexist to assume that women are biologically determined to continue performing this work. An adequate political theory must evaluate traditional sexual, childbearing and childrearing practices and consider more liberatory alternatives. (Pp. 112–113)

Feminists critique the existing liberal political and economic theory that separates the public and private and that makes a distinction between the public "economic world of the market" and the private, "noneconomic" sphere of the home. The distinction is value laden and has been used to rationalize the exploitation of women (Jaggar, 1983). Women's labor is crucial in enhancing social, economic, and political development of any state in the public sphere.

Critics question the universality of the public/private distinctions. Stamp (1989) argues that the assumed Western conceptualization of the public/private dichotomies of "human existence" is an inaccurate conceptualization of present and, even more so, past African life. She points out that Western notions of public and private distinctions cannot be used to understand African communities. Stamp argues that the community of most African women is as full a participant in the decision-making structure of village life as is the community of men. She argues that women's voices are silent, not because they participate only in the private sphere but due to the privileged status of the community of men gained through contemporary socioeconomic processes. Stamp posits that, although women are largely absent from contemporary national and "formal" political institutions, their political efficacy continues to be manifested at the community level. Amadiume (1989) argues that the assumption that the domestic/public dichotomy that led a group of high-powered female anthropologists in the United States to the conclusion that maternal and domestic roles were responsible for the supposed universal subordination of women is an ethnocentric view (p. 4).

In a study that is set within a postcolonial context, the public and private distinctions are useful in understanding and differentiating the nature of the public or formal sphere where policies are formulated and of the private sphere where rural women's agency is confined. Women are largely absent at the contemporary national level where policies are formulated. The women's discourses at the local level, though public at the community level as exemplified by their activities as individuals and as collectives, do not inform the larger "authentic" or legitimated discourses that are articulated in policy documents. Van Allen (1976) argues for a notion of public that relates to the collectivity of decision making where a few individuals may possess the knowledge required to make decisions at the public level. He notes that:

> The settling of questions that concern the welfare of the community in a "public" way necessitates the sharing of "political knowledge"—the knowledge needed for participation in political discussion and decision. A system in which public policy is made publicly and the relevant knowledge is shared widely contrasts sharply with those systems in which a privileged few possess the relevant knowledge—whether priestly mysteries or bureaucratic expertise—and therefore control policy decisions. (Quoted in Stamp, 1989, p. 115)

The nature of collectivity, and the space or style in which that collectivity operates, are important distinctions of public and private spheres. In Kenya, women operate in the spheres that have been rendered less visible by contemporary male-dominated structures and discourses. Inevitably, the community of men has been favored over the community of women. Men have had the privilege of making decisions at the public level that affect all people. In the African context, these public/private distinctions have taken root because:

> Outsiders, from missionaries to colonial officials to contemporary governmental elite, have recognized men's networks as

the sole, legitimate "public" with which they should deal—the uniform, undifferentiated "public" that embodies "public" interest. (Stamp, 1989, p. 116)

Public discourse articulated in policy documents is produced and disseminated mainly by the community of men in the contemporary state through state-sponsored strategies. It is the legitimate and dominant discourse on education. The private discourses on education produced by women are produced mostly at the individual level, and to a lesser extent, at the group level. The women's discourses are primarily their lived experiences existing at the "private/informal" world of "women's affairs." However, discourse is not neutral. As Apple (1991, Introduction to Lather, 1991) points out, "all our discourses are politically uninnocent and occur within shifting and dynamic social context in which the existence of multiple sets of power [and gender relations] are inevitable" (p. vii). Power, Foucault (1980b) argues, is not a property but a strategy that is constantly in tension and in activity. Consequently, public and private discourses on education interact in complex ways. We see this exemplified in the Kilome women's actions in shaping and transforming their children and particularly, their daughters' experiences of educational and development policies produced at the national level. The women are not mere victims of public policy discourses, but they act upon these policies as individuals and as collectives. They interact within the constraints and opportunities of existing structures at the same time as they act upon and restructure the social system.

The study upon which this book is based involves women at the grassroots level. Stamp (1986) describes these women as the backbone of the Kenyan peasantry who are doubly dominated as peasants within underdeveloped capitalism and as a dominated category within the peasantry. Despite the crucial role that these women play in the society, their realities have continued to be invisible in public discourses covering all aspects of the society, and specifically, in the education discourse in Kenya. Freire (1990) argues that "reality" is never simply an objective datum, or a concrete fact, but is also certain people's perception of it because of the indispensable unity between subjectivity and objectivity in the act of knowing. Reality is not independent of our experiences, and thus social, economic, cultural, and political factors play a major role in shaping people's reality. The reality of women and men's lives is shaped by the complex interactions of the social, political, economic, cultural, and historical contexts of the particular society.

Feminists have shown that women's experiences have either been ignored or distorted (Eichler, 1983, p. 60; Harding, 1986). More importantly, Eurocentricity, and the desire by Western feminists to use Western values as yardsticks, have produced the "Third World woman" as a singular monolithic subject—a stereotype that has worked to her detriment (Amadiume, 1989; Mohanty, 1991). Kenyan women's delineation of their reality from these perspectives is important in countering the hegemonic perceptions of women that have portrayed them as stereotypical pawns of men.

Stamp (1995) argues that a text on African women's agency must ask new questions, ones that aim to elicit what women are doing as active agents of resistance and change in the maelstrom of contemporary African affairs. Potash (1989), writing about gender relations in African societies, argues that it is crucial that we begin to ask questions that clarify the complexities of women and men's relationships—questions that portray the "reality" of women's lives as social actors who use systems to achieve their ends. Potash concludes that "such praxis approaches emphasize human resourcefulness while recognizing systemic limitations" (p. 191).

Ahlberg-Maina (1991) concurs with Stamp and Potash about the importance of taking African women as actors contrary to the passive image of African women portrayed in most contemporary literature. In her study of the response of women's groups to family-planning programs in Kenya, Ahlberg-Maina used the actor-systems-dynamics analytical framework to understand women's experiences. "The actor-systems-dynamics approach recognizes the dynamics of social actors whether individuals or collectives in social structuration and transformation" (p. 32). She argues that women are social actors who formulate strategies aimed at influencing or shaping the social system. She notes that, as social actors, women are engaged in the making of their own history, a process that is not only continuous, but one where past experiences, knowledge, and cultural traits are carried along. Ahlberg-Maina concludes that, even as a dominated group, women are a dynamic force in the shaping of the social system. This strategy makes visible the different forms of struggle and resistance that women engage in during their daily lives. It also challenges the racist, sexist, and superiority notions that have been embedded in anthropological and sociological studies on African/Black and Third World women (Amadiume, 1989).

Women interact within the constraints and opportunities of existing structures at the same time as they act upon and restructure the social system. This women's agency resides in their individual and communal endeavors and is constantly reinvented in the context of political and social change (Stamp, 1995).

For the women's agency to become visible, they must participate in the study as who they really are—subjects and knowers as Harding (1986) emphasizes rather than as the objects of study that has been the pattern in many conventional research methodologies. As knowers, the women participate in knowledge production through participation, dialogue, and analyses of discourses/discussions (Fals-Borda & Rahman, 1991). The women not only participated as knowers and subjects, but their voices as subjects of inquiry, and the voice of the inquirer are culturally identifiable. This created the possibility of understanding the women's condition as well as my own from the standpoint of historically and culturally locatable experiences (Smith, 1987).

Many research methodologists, particularly postpositivists, advocate reciprocity of research. Lather (1986) argues that participants should gain self-understanding and, ideally, self-determination through the research. The methodology of this study made reciprocity a viable objective. The women's understanding of the dynamics of gender inequities in accessing educational opportunities and self-determination is evident in the goals of the women's self-help groups, in both old and newly formed groups, and in the systematic progress that the women have made in achieving these goals. The women's actions as a group, and as individuals, have created the possibility for the transformation of their own and of their children's world or "reality." The research process has contributed to the reorientation, focus, and energization of participants in what Freire (1990) termed *conscientization,* knowing reality in order to better transform it. Mies (1983) argues that active collective consciousness becomes possible only when women can use their own documented (spoken), understood, and analyzed history as a "weapon" in the struggle for themselves.

Mies also notes the importance of creating a wider network of communication for women from different villages or cities. She argues that a research project should be linked to an ongoing movement. Mies argues that "a research project that does not link up with some local group which can become a permanent base for conscientization, mobilization and action will remain at best a pleasant episode in the lives of the women" (p. 137).

Smith (1987) observes that research *for* women must begin from the standpoints of women. Such an inquiry regards women's experience as starting and ending points for inquiry. Alcoff (1991) states that anyone who speaks for others should only do so out of a concrete analysis of the particular power relations and discursive effects involved. Roman (1993) argues that "the concept of *speaking with* conveys the possibility of tendential and shifting alliances between speakers from different unequally located groups" (p. 184, italics added). I struggle to speak with the women while being conscious of Alcoff's cautions on the problematic of speaking for and about others.

Feminism as a political movement struggles for methodologies that can bring women's experiences to light and put such experiences on the political agenda (Mies, 1983). What I have striven for are methodologies that are informed by epistemologies that consider women as knowers and active agents of social change, not as mere victims. These methodologies must also consider gender, race, class, and ethnicity as vital categories of analysis in understanding women's material standpoints.

The complexities of feminism as a political movement aimed at addressing women's issues are intensified by the fact that the female subject is herself a site of differences. Mohanty (1991) takes Western feminists to task for having asked the wrong questions and thereby producing "the Third World woman" as a singular monolithic subject. Mohanty posits:

> Assumptions of privilege and ethnocentric universality, on the one hand, and inadequate self-consciousness about the effect of Western scholarship on "third world" in the context of a world system dominated by the West, on the other, characterize a sizable extent of Western feminist work on women in the third world. . . . Marginal or not, this writing has political effects and implications beyond the immediate feminist or disciplinary audience. (P. 53)

The consequences of the distortion of women's lives have been reflected in the development enterprise discourse and in policies on Third World women. Discourses ranging from academic writing to the design, implementation, and monitoring of aid projects by public and private agencies reaffirm a view of African women as passive, problematic targets of benevolent intervention (Stamp, 1995). Davies and Graves (1986) argue that the portrayal of the African woman as a supermother, as a symbol of Africa, or as the one with a golden heart does not necessarily counter the facile racist image of African women portrayed in many anthropological studies (Amadiume, 1989). Davies and Graves argue "for a truthful assessment of women's lives, the negative and the positive and a demonstration of the specific choices that women must often make" (p. 15). In addition, Amadiume notes that work by Third World women must be political, challenging the new and growing patriarchal systems imposed on our societies through colonialism and Western religious and educational influences (p. 9). Countering the racist and sexist discourses on African women involves making visible women's resistance as well as their compliance with the patriarchal structures that perpetuate their subordination. As Van Maanen (1988) argues, ethnographies are politically mediated, since the power of one group or researcher to represent another is always involved. Most crucially, ethnography irrevocably influences the interests and lives of the people represented in them both individually and collectively, for better or for worse.

Guided by this framework, aware of my own privileges of educational and socioeconomic status, I entered the lives of the women of Kilome division to talk with them about their experience with the educational system. I worked with the women in their capacities as daughters, sisters, mothers, and/or wives. I used gender as a category of analysis because:

Insofar as women and men have been shown to participate differently in the economic, social, political,[education] and religious life of their societies, we cannot continue to describe institutions as if they are gender neutral when they are not. Rather, an understanding of social organization and social process requires new conceptualizations that use gender as an integral theme of analysis, not as a marginal category. By focusing on participatory patterns and the diverse interests and strategies of women and men we obtain a more realistic picture. Furthermore, since the allocation of rights and responsibilities among men and women have implications for their relationship to one another and to their society, such analyses hold promise for improving our understanding of gender systems. (Potash, 1989, p. 189)

Research Design

Harding (1986) points out that "method" deals with "techniques for gathering evidence" while "methodology" is a "theory and analysis of how research does or should proceed" (pp. 2–3). In order to make visible the gender and power issues that limit women's participation in education, the economy, and the wider Kenya society, it became important to involve the women, particularly those living in the rural areas. These women's struggles to participate in Kenyan society are exacerbated by the limited educational opportunities made available to them and by the rural-urban dichotomy in the development of the formal employment sector. I chose to interview women who were born, raised, and who received part of their formal education in Kilome division, Makueni District, Kenya. I interviewed women about their experiences of formal education, highlighting the barriers that they faced in accessing educational opportunities as well as their daughters' limitations to educational and economic opportunities. The women's narratives represent their private discourse on education that I use to discuss the public discourse on the role of education in development articulated in policy documents.

I also examined the policy documents produced over the last thirty-year period in light of the political, social, and economic rhetoric of the time. All of the policy documents represent the government's position on the role of education in development. I examined the public discourse on education to understand the rationale for providing educational opportunities. I was interested in finding out whether there is a commitment to providing women with educational opportunities equal to those of their male counterparts or whether women are only provided educational opportunities sufficient for improving the delivery of services as mothers and/or wives in the private sphere. This analysis reveals the gendered and cultural assumptions of femininity and masculinity legitimated at the public national level. In addition, analyzing policy documents contextualizes the women's interviews and provides a better understanding of their subjectivities and subordination. It also makes visible how policies have limited, and continue to limit, women's agency in the public sphere.

Interviewing

The major data collection strategy in the field was semistructured open-ended interviews. As Reinharz (1992) points out, this type of research makes it possible to explore people's views of reality from which theory may be generated. With the women in rural areas and in Salama, I conducted the interviews in the local dialect of Kikamba, a variant of the Bantu language. I used a mixture of Kikamba, Swahili, and English with the professional women.[2] Holding interviews in a mixture of the three languages was an advantage because there are certain words that attain their full meanings, strength, and flavor only if expressed in the vernacular. Being a Muûkamba and one who grew up in this area, I had an added advantage in that I could understand the proverbs and idioms that the women used, as well as the nuances that characterized their way of talking. Laughter among Kamba women is a communicative tool. There are certain ways in which women can laugh to imply, for example, "subversiveness" on their part. It would be difficult for one who did not grow up in the village to understand these nuances.

Translation of Interviews

In order to write this ethnography I have had to translate the interviews from Kikamba and Kiswahili into English. Aware that advantages of interviewing in vernacular would be compromised during translations, I tried to get clarifications from the women of the specific meaning of words that they used that I felt would be hard to translate into English. Asking the women questions like "What do you mean by that?" and "Please explain further" helped me during my translation of the interviews from Kikamba into English. Since language is dynamic, it was important for me to seek elaboration on words and phrases that were not familiar to me because the Kikamba language is laden with metaphors that can be altered to suit specific situations.

While writing this ethnography, I have continued to examine my translations of the interview, seeking ways of improving them. I have sought my husband's knowledge of Kikamba and compared my interpretations of certain words and phrases with his. His assistance has helped me to represent the women's voices as accurately as possible, given my limitations and including the fact that English is my third language after Swahili!

Writing Ethnography

Culture is not itself visible but is made visible through its representation. Ethnography, the result of fieldwork, is the written report that represents the culture. Writing ethnographies is not unproblematic (Van Maanen, 1988). Gluck and Patai (1991) point out, moreover, that "women interviewing women is not an unproblematic activity either. Taping a woman's words, asking appropriate questions, laughing at the right moment, displaying empathy—these are not enough" (p. 9). Anderson and Jack (1991) argue that for women-interviewers to hear women's perspectives accurately:

We have to learn to listen in stereo, receiving both the dominant and muted channels clearly and tuning into them care-
fully to understand the relationship between them . . . search
for stories that lie beyond constraints of acceptable discussion
to the experience that lies outside the boundaries of accept-
ability. (P. 11)

Stacey (1991) argues that there is dissonance between fieldwork
practice and the ethnographic product. She argues that "despite
the fact that ethnographic methods place the researcher and the
informants in a collaborative, reciprocal quest for understanding,
the research product is ultimately that of the researcher, however
modified or influenced it may be by informants" (p. 114). Even
though representing others is problematic, representation of others
still remains crucial in the struggle for political and cultural empowerment for those groups who have remained silenced, due to
specific material, intellectual, and social circumstances (Salazar,
1991).
    I am conscious of the contradictions of writing an ethnography
of the women of Kilome. On the one hand lies the potential for
exploitation, and on the other hand is the crucial role that this
ethnography contributes to understanding gender relations in African societies, specifically: making visible women's agency in the midst
of harsh economic, social, and political contexts. Writing this ethnography is important since it makes their agency beyond motherhood
visible. Consequently, Kilome women's discourses on education are
"constructed" from interviews that I held with them as individuals
and as a group. The discourses are constructed by putting gender at
the center of the women's experiences. "Feminist researchers see
gender as a basic organizing principle which profoundly shapes and/
or mediates the concrete conditions of our lives" (Lather, 1991, p.
17). The women's experiences are structured by gendered assumptions within different historical, cultural, economic, and political
contexts of Kenyan society. The ethnography I am writing is influenced
by what Lather calls "postpositivists' emancipatory approaches to
inquiry" with feminist approaches playing a major role.

Reflections on Doing Research in Kilome Division

Scheurich (1997) argues that, "contrary to the fact that many, widely
differing kinds of validity have been delineated across a burgeon-
ing array of research paradigms, the myriad kinds of validity are

simply masks that conceal a profound and disturbing sameness" (p. 1). He notes that validity wears different epistemological masks, and he concludes that validity as a practice across both conventional and postpositivist paradigms is a civilization project, a bifurcation reinscribing dominance of the Same over the Other. He advocates for "the validity of *voice* which does not prevent the innumerable voices of difference from participating equitably in the conversations of human kinds which is based on the fact that the researcher is researching those from her or his own social location" (p. 19, italics added).

My fieldwork took me back to the village where I was born and raised. Reflecting on my entry into the research field, I realize that I had to begin to think and act like one of the women of Kilome, a Muûkamba woman, the ethnic group to which these women and I belong. I had to learn how to create a comfortable atmosphere for these women. This involved abandoning the linear method of inquiry.

When women meet, they must share some food or a cup of tea. It is the Akamba belief that a host does not ask for a story (or questions) of their guest before he or she feeds them. For this reason, I had to make tea and prepare food for the more than one hundred and twenty women who met with me at various times during the fieldwork.

I learned from these women that I could not maintain a sequence of discussing their educational experiences, for instance, it became clear that women were not preoccupied with why they left school. It was obvious that they had left school, but their major interest was to begin talking about possibilities—their agency and using the past to inform the present. The women gave me the message that they are living in the present and not in the past.

Barriers and Dilemmas

My age and education, at times, became barriers that had to be overcome for the women to tell their stories, for example, there were silences when I introduced the topic of sexuality. I attributed this silence to the fact that sexuality is seen as a taboo topic that should be handled in private. Traditionally, youngsters of a particular age group (teenagers) learned about sexuality from "experts" prior to their circumcision. Our group discussions involved women of various ages. During these discussions, the young women did not feel free to discuss sexuality in the presence of the older women. The latter, however, seemed to have fewer difficulties talking about their sexuality. This is not surprising because, culturally, it was the older women, particularly grandmothers, who discussed aspects of female sexuality with their granddaughters.

Being partly an insider and relatively young was also a dilemma. The older women maintained the image of me as a child; they kept their image of me "frozen" in the past. This perception of me as a child provides an explanation for the times when there would be prolonged silence from the women. I was able to diffuse their "frozen" image of me by invoking our shared experiences, particularly motherhood and wifehood. My children's presence reminded them that I was no longer a child. Often, I asked the oldest women to share with us how they have handled men. I suggested that it was important for us younger women to hear how our mothers worked their way around patriarchy. To gain their trust, I stressed our commonality. I was particularly amazed at how older women have used sexuality to get their husbands' attention. These strategies proved to be important ways of breaking the silence.

Although there were benefits of being a local "girl," there were also special tensions that arose as a result of this factor. The local member of parliament and his stalwarts could not believe that my research was not a cover-up for soliciting votes. Because rural people have the votes, politicians in Kenya are concerned when those they perceive as potential competitors, professionals, establish a relationship with the people at the grassroots level. My actions were interpreted as a preparation for the 1997 parliamentary elections. This rumor culminated in a visit meeting by a man from the Criminal Investigation Department (CID). He was interested in knowing why the women met and if their meetings were authorized. The visit enraged the women, and they categorically refused to be harassed and intimidated by him. An older woman, a petty trader, confronted the special branch officer and insisted that women's self-help groups were not a new phenomenon and indeed that their group had authorization to meet. She insisted that his visit was designed to intimidate women so that the group would collapse. She had the support of all the other women. The women challenged the man to sit down and listen to issues they were discussing. Since he could not take the challenge, he excused himself and left.

Rumors of what would be done to women who were found holding political gatherings under the guise of women's self-help groups did intimidate some women. Indeed some of the women were "forced" to reevaluate their membership. Some even stopped attending the meetings as a result of the visit by the CID official, as they feared what would happen to them if they were arrested. A week later, the chairperson of this group was called to Kilome, the divisional headquarters of the Office of the President, to explain the purpose of the group. She was accused of being a leader of a gang of women who do not know how to speak to men! This was because the man was challenged by women, an unacceptable reaction in a gender-stratified society.

The local MP, who has a grade 6 education, certainly felt that if I declared my interest in his constituency, I would have a large following since he had not lived up to his campaign promises, and he was not making any effort to reach the people at the grassroots level who voted him into parliament. The fact that I was working closely with the women was a threat to him, as he did not have a similar relationship with his electorate, the majority of whom are women, since so many men work away from the area. My attempts to bridge the gap between myself as an educated person and as a woman with women in the grassroots level were construed as political and subversive. Demystification of power relations between researchers and the researched and social change are some of the aims of feminist research.

My work with the women of Kilome division made me aware of the importance of hearing the voices of the subjects of your study. Even though I was born, raised, and partly schooled in Kilome division I could not pretend to know the experiences of these women. I thought I understood life in Kilome; I thought I knew all the issues, and I thought I knew why women dropped out of school. My conversations with the women showed me that my awareness of their issues was both superficial and stereotypical. I needed to hear from the women if I were to begin to write anything about their educational experiences. I became aware of the exclusion of rural women's concerns and needs from the public discourses on education and development that affect their lives and those of their children, for example, women had no access to information on how to access government support for their children's education or to get credit to improve their income-generating activities. As time passed and as the women's list of required information grew, I began to understand why one woman had said to me "maybe you are an angel sent to help us penetrate this labyrinth."

In summary, I sought a methodology that would enable the women to articulate their experiences and to identify issues that limited their participation in education, in employment and in other social activities and how these factors have shaped and continue to shape their daily experiences. It had to be one that would empower the women and demystify the power relations invariably involved in research. The research methodology made women's agency visible as social actors who formulate strategies for influencing and shaping the social system of which they are a part.

5

Analyses of Education- and Development-Policy Documents

*It is 10:30 A.M. and a bell rings to mark the end of the first session
of the school day. Kids dash out of classes like winged termites after a
heavy downpour. A group of girls are jumping a sisal rope,
another group of boys are playing with a ball made from sisal pith.
Close by is another group of girls, 8–10 years old.
They are singing, singing a "mature" song.*

*Niw'aa nanonie nditinda ndilumangwa,
ningusyoka kwitu ngatwawe nula ngwenda
ninguvoya Ngai ni syae twana twili
Kala ka kavisi ndiketa Tom Mboya
Kala ka kelitu ni Ngina wa Kenyatta*
or
*I have taken enough beatings
I will go back to my home and get married to a man of my choice
I will pray God to give me two children
I will call the boy Tom Mboya
I will call the girl Ngina Kenyatta*

What does this song have to do with policy? Who was Tom Mboya and who was Ngina Kenyatta? Why would children from the Kamba ethnic group in Ukambani, the region where I did my fieldwork, want to name their children after these two people from the Luo and Kikuyu ethnic groups? Why would they break their Kamba-naming customs and name their children after some man and woman from a different ethnic group? What did Tom Mboya and Ngina Kenyatta symbolize?

Tom Mboya symbolized the model politician, freedom fighter, and elite policy maker. He was the first minister for economic planning and development in independent Kenya and a nationalist, his popularity transversing the forty-six ethnic groups of Kenya. He was assassinated in 1969. His popularity was perceived as a threat to the presidency of Mzee Jomo Kenyatta, the first president of independent Kenya.

Ngina Kenyatta, the wife of Mzee Jomo Kenyatta, was referred to as the mother of the nation—Mama (mother) Ngina Kenyatta. She was the president's third wife, a "gift" to him from the Kikuyu, the president's ethnic group. She was young and he was old. The president's ability to father children at his advanced age was a source of pride for the old man and one he boasted of when he addressed the nation during national holidays.

Three decades after independence, policy-making is still predominantly a male preserve. The public discourse regarding the purpose of education of women and men in Kenya is set out predominantly by male politicians and policy makers. Most women continue with their reproductive and productive roles in the private sphere as mothers, wives, daughters, sisters, care givers, and petty traders. These women's work go unnoticed and their concerns remain invisible.

This chapter is an analysis of Kenya government educational policy recommendation reports, which represent the public or official discourse on education in Kenya. I examine the official discourse on education as a state apparatus (Dale, 1989) set within the development discourse of Kenya and its impact on the education of women in Kenya.

Education assumes a central role in development plans in Kenya as in many other countries. Peatie (1981), upon reviewing the history of development planning since the mid-twentieth century concluded that "the planning of education has been placed squarely and legitimately into development planning" (quoted in Thomas, 1992, p. 17). Government-initiated development plans in Kenya are influenced by international development agencies such as the World Bank and the International Monetary Fund (IMF) whose operations are perceived as far from being politically neutral by most members of less developed countries (Brett, 1983). The education portion of national development plans typically assigns to the education system roles and responsibilities that will contribute to the national development goals and suggests ways in which the system should be improved so that the roles may be performed more efficiently (Thomas, 1992).

Unlike in the colonial times before independence in 1963, Kenyan policymakers have had the opportunity to formulate policies to enhance the social, economic, and political development of their country. Under colonial power, the people of Kenya had no voice in government; the nation's natural resources were organized and developed mainly for the benefit of non-Africans; and the nation's human resources remained largely uneducated, untrained, inexperienced, and deprived of the economic benefits of their labor (Wanjigi Report, 1983).

As Freire (1985) argues, education is not a neutral enterprise; it is political throughout. The colonial government had used education to enhance and to maintain a racially segregated society, and to regulate access to economic, political, and social opportunities, consequently limiting Africans to occupations of a rural, semitribal society and to the lowest levels of the public administration (Ominde, 1964).

At independence, education became an arm of the Kenya nation—a new notion within which, as the new leaders claimed, all people had equal rights. Education was pressed into service to help to foster the psychological basis of nationhood, to promote national unity, and to serve as an instrument for the conscious change of attitudes. Leaders in independent Kenya had been witnesses to the power of education in the control of social, economic, and political opportunities during the colonial period. Consequently, the government assumed central responsibility for education at all levels by removing responsibility from various communal and religious bodies who managed the segregated system (Gachathi, 1976).

Since independence, the government's control of education has been enshrined in the Laws of Kenya under the Education Act. This act entrusts the minister of education with the responsibility of promoting the education of "the people of Kenya and the progressive development of institutions devoted to the promotion of education" (Republic of Kenya, Laws of Kenya: Education Act 1980, p. 5). The minister is also "in charge of securing the effective co-operation, under his [sic] general direction or control, of all public bodies concerned with education in carrying out the national policy for education" (p. 5). The Education Act "allows the Minister to order or entrust any of his functions with respect to education to a local authority on such terms, conditions or restrictions he think[s] fit" (p. 6).

Involvement of the public is sought during the formulation of educational policy recommendations. Often educators, parents, community leaders, and the general public are invited for interviews and their submissions are welcomed. Consequently, the "unofficial" voices are given an opportunity to contribute to the national discourse on education. Whether their views have any impact on the educational guidelines that result from these commissions is another issue.

I examine briefly the following government-initiated educational and development reports that have been produced over the last thirty years: the Ominde Report (1964), the Gachathi Report (1976), the Mackay Report (1981), the Wanjigi Report (1982–1983), the Kamunge Report (1988), and the Ndegwa Report (1991). These reports give a picture of the pattern of changes in educational policies in Kenya since independence in 1963 to the present. The policies have been used as guidelines in the formulation of relevant curricula. Downey (1988) argues that "policy is an instrument of governance and policy making involves the processing of needs and demands of society as well as establishing of guidelines for the functioning of the system" (p. 23).

The Ominde Report was the first educational document for independent Kenya. Ominde educational policy recommendations set the path for formal Western education in independent Kenya. New educational policies were recommended to press education into the service of Africans/Kenyans and to afford them academic educational opportunities denied them in the previous colonial African education system. The Gachathi Report examined the impact of the educational policies implemented at independence on national development. The Mackay Report was the third major educational policy recommendation report. It examined the education system with a specific mandate of laying policy directions for the establishment of a second university after Nairobi University. Closely following the Mackay Report was the Wanjigi Report that examined education's role in the quest for solutions to the unemployment problem in Kenya. The Wanjigi Report endorsed the Mackay Report's recommendations of restructuring the entire education system as a strategy for combating unemployment. The Kamunge Report reviewed national education and training for the next decade and beyond. The latest policy document, the Ndegwa Report, addressed unemployment in Kenya, both in the short and long term.

I also examine the policy document entitled "Sessional Paper # 10 of 1965." It was derived from the Kenya African National Union (KANU)[1] Manifesto of 1963. This document adopted and entrenched colonial (European) concepts of individualism exemplified in individual male property ownership. Property ownership and specifically land ownership vests in individuals the power to enter into social relations on the basis and extent of their property (Dale, 1989). As education has become central to national development plans, I also analyze the education sections in the 1974–1978 and 1989–1993 development plans.

I analyze the policy documents in light of the political, social, and economic rhetoric of the time. This involves examining the public discourse in relation to the following: the role of education in national development, women's education including access and barriers, women and the economy, and women and the family.

I examine the public discourse on education for the rationale for providing women with educational opportunities. Whether there has been a commitment to providing women with educational and economic opportunities equal to those of their male counterparts or whether educational opportunities for women have been merely part of improving the delivery of services as mothers and/or wives in the private sphere is of importance. This examination makes visible the gendered and cultural assumptions of femininity and masculinity legitimated at the public national level. In conclusion, I examine the shifting policy themes and the treatment of gender in the policy documents since independence. I analyzed the policy documents chronologically beginning with the Ominde Report.

Ominde Report (1964)

The Ominde Report (1964) was produced by the Kenya Education Commission, which was initiated by the president of Kenya a week after independence, on 19 December 1963. This commission was composed of fourteen members—thirteen men and one woman—all of whom were appointed by the minister of education. The commission was chaired by Prof. Simeon H. Ominde, one of the few Africans to hold academic credentials at the time. Four commissioners were members of parliament, others were high-ranking civil servants, and some were academics. The sole female member was not an academic or a politician. She participated in the panel that examined primary level education.

The commission had the task of formulating policies on education to serve the new Kenyan nation. Previous colonial policies dealt with education as separate social activities along racial lines as European education, Asian education, and African education. Africans were given an education deemed suitable to their position in colonial life and "appropriate" to the African population, the lowest echelons of the society. Colonial policy on the education of Africans ensured the most of the African population had little or no education.

Members of the public were invited to present written and oral submissions to the commission. This invitation gave educators, critics, and other members of the public an opportunity to express their views. Although the commissioners claimed that their net was flung widely and that they sought, and obtained, a great deal of information about the thinking of people in all parts of the country on educational problems, the final policy recommendations were their sole responsibility.

The Ominde Report noted the crucial role that education had to play in the cultural, social, economic, and political development of the newfound nation of Kenya. Kenya was in a period of multiple transitions from a subsistence to a monetary economy, from the development of natural and human resources for others to the development of these resources for the benefit of Kenya (Ominde, 1964). The report noted that a highly skilled *African* labor force was required not only to take up positions that had previously been occupied by Europeans and Asians but also to meet the nation's economic development. The Ominde Report recommended the provision of universal basic education and production of high-level *African* skilled human resource for cultural, economic, and political reasons. Education in newfound Kenya was set to foster a sense of nationhood and national unity, serve all Kenyans without discrimination, promote social equality and remove divisions of *race, tribe,* and *religion,* and respect the cultural traditions of the peoples of Kenya, both as expressed in social institutions and relationships (Ominde, 1964, p. 25, italics added). Consequently, the education system was placed into the service of achieving the social, cultural, economic, and political goals of a newly independent nation.

At the eve of independence, women were underrepresented in education in Kenya since education was developed by the colonial administrators along gender and racial lines. The Ominde Report rejected appeals for girls-only boarding primary schools. Advocates of those schools had argued that "in mixed schools their [girls'] interests are neglected, that they are used by teachers for the performance of duties unrelated to the classroom, and even that there are moral dangers in mixed education at the upper primary age" (p. 65). The report argued that providing boarding primary schools for girls only would not be expensive but would not necessarily solve the problems identified by proponents of single-sex schools. The report, however, recommended single-sex secondary schools as requested by a large number of heads of schools who made oral submissions to the commission. The Ominde Report noted that the need to Kenyanize or to Africanize the entire infrastructure of the modern work force, particularly management positions, demanded quick production of highly skilled African manpower [sic] from a pool of uneducated Africans. "The African majority, under colonial rule, had been left with educational prospects which, despite popular pressure, were limited by sheer numbers, by the modest means placed at their disposal and by the social and occupational role to which they were restricted" (p. 21).

In short, the commissioner did not seek to replace the colonial education offered in Kenya prior to independence. Rather, they sought to change the rules that regulated the educational opportunities to favor the "African-Kenyan." The category of race eclipsed other forms of inequalities that were part of the inherited colonial system of education and governance. Policy recommendations zeroed in on race issues such as the Africanization of the modern sector. Subtly, the education system after independence negated the existence of gender barriers in access to educational opportunities and employment opportunities. In addition, the Ominde Report emphasized academic education as a prerequisite for participation in the formal/modern employment sector, and emphasized the modern sector that is urban based. This approach accelerated the rural-urban migration of mostly male job seekers.

Sessional Paper # 10: African Socialism and Its Application to Planning Policy (1965)

The Sessional # 10: African Socialism and Its Application to Planning Policy document was produced in 1965, approximately eighteen months after independence. It was an in-depth elaboration of the principles of the Democratic African Socialist State as per declarations in the KANU Manifesto of 1963. The KANU Manifesto was a set of declarations that were adopted by the government of Kenya at independence, to provide guidance in its approach to social, economic, and political developmental matters.

The sessional paper emphasized rapid economic growth as the guiding principle upon which all policies in independent Kenya would be made and implemented. Rapid economic growth was seen as a solution to the social, economic, and political difficulties that Kenya was facing. In this paper, the government noted that a highly skilled human resource and new property laws were necessary to enhance economic development.

Education was seen as much, or more, of an economic service rather than a social service. It was a principal means for relieving the shortage of a domestic skilled work force and equalizing economic opportunities among all citizens and for the acceleration of Africanization. Production of high-skilled human resource was seen as a major factor to enhance economic growth. The government warned that free education could not be provided at the expense of economic growth. It also warned that no individual or group would be permitted to exert undue influence on policies of the state. It was made clear that "the State, was never to become the tool of special interests, catering to the desires of a minority at the expense of the needs of the majority" (Sessional Paper # 10, 1965, p. 3).

The government argued that Kenya was in a transition from a subsistence economy to a monetary economy and needed to mobilize resources to attain a rapid rate of economic growth. This economic mobilization and reorganization of resources needed planning, direction, control, and cooperation. It was pointed out that:

> Kenya is in a period of multiple transition set in motion by the attainment of Independence. We are in transition from a subsistence to a monetary economy, from an *economic dependence on agriculture* to a more balanced growth, from a development of human and natural resources for the benefit of the people of Kenya. (Sessional Paper # 10, 1965, p. 1, italics added)

Selected language was used to make Kenyans feel that the changes made were for their good. Ensuing policies, particularly those that dealt with property (land) ownership and the government's perceptions of equity issues denied women social, economic, and political rights.

In precolonial Kenya, land was essentially communally or tribally owned. In this period, land registration policy was introduced. This policy was reinforced in postcolonial Kenya. During this time, Kenyans were warned that traditional attitudes toward rights to land would not be carried over to a modern, monetary economy. It was pointed out that "a credit economy rests heavily on a system of land titles and registration and, ownership of land must, therefore, be made more definite and explicit if land consolidation and development are to be fully successful" (Sessional Paper # 10, 1965, pp. 10–11). The "new" meanings of ownership, adopted from the colonialists, emphasized the individual rather than communal ownership and encouraged and facilitated the transfer of property from the community to individuals. Consequently, land was registered under the name of the head of the household or a male relative. This greatly limited women's access to land. The issuance of land title deeds to men as heads of households gave, and still gives, men absolute control over the use of the land including the disposal of the land against the will of the wife and children.

The paper also repudiated the existence of classism in Kenya. It claimed that the sharp class division that existed in Europe had no parallel in African society and no place in "African socialism,"[2] which was the public political perspective at that time. The document stated that no class problem arose in the traditional African society and none exists today among Africans (Sessional Paper # 10, 1965). The paper did not discuss gender issues. However, the recommended policy directions impacted men and women, and the rich and the poor differently.

1974-1978 Development Plan

The 1974–1978 Development Plan defined the economic, social, and political context within which the Gachathi Report was realized in 1976. The plan gave the directions and limits within which policy recommendations were to be made so that national needs were not jeopardized. Economic development was the central theme of this development plan.

Ten years after independence, the country had failed to attain rapid economic growth due to external and internal factors. Internally, there was a political crisis as leaders questioned the interpretations of "African socialism" by the president of Kenya. Such leaders included Ja Ramogi Oginga Odinga who had resigned his position as the country's vice president because he felt that the ideals of "African socialism" had been violated and replaced with those of Western capitalism. Kenya also had to address the challenges of a high unemployment rate, an education and economic system that promoted rural-urban migration, high population growth, and high costs of educating Kenyans particularly at higher levels of education. Educational changes had to be instituted not only to cope with the sluggish economy but also to stimulate its growth. These included curriculum changes from an emphasis on academic to vocational education, and reduction of government spending on education and the introduction of the cost-sharing strategy. As Dale (1989) argues, demands for education to become more economically relevant become louder when the economy is doing badly (p. 95).

The plan recommended the introduction of applied subjects into secondary schools in an effort to provide primary and secondary school graduates with skills needed by the Kenya economy. Vocational education was seen as capable of solving the unemployment problem by providing graduates with the necessary skills needed in industry and also for self-employment. As a result the rural-urban migration could be curbed through the creation of jobs in rural areas and by making rural areas more attractive places to live and work. Nevertheless, the vocational education offered was limited by the lack of physical facilities (workshops and equipment) and by areas of concentration. Courses offered were woodwork, masonry, carpentry, and tailoring. These are gender-specific courses that gave boys more opportunities than girls. The potential for self-employment was further curtailed by a lack of resources to purchase tools and equipment.

Recommendations were made in the 1974–1978 Development Plan to introduce cost sharing at the secondary and tertiary levels of education. Kenyans had to take more responsibility for educating themselves. The independence promises of provision of free education to Kenyans changed to reflect the prevailing economic circumstances. It was argued that education was no longer a right but a privilege, as well as a scarce item. Each one who had access to education was warned to "occupy his time wisely and learn as much as he can for his own benefit and for the greater future of his nation" (1974–1978 Development Plan, p. 22).

The cost-sharing strategy proposed in this plan demanded that parents increase their financial participation in their children's education through the payment of tuition and nontuition fees. This strategy increased limitations on girls' education and economic opportunities because when resources are scarce parents are more likely to invest in the education of boys than that of girls due to cultural-gendered assumptions surrounding masculinity and femininity. This plan, however, did not address the impact of a cost-sharing strategy within a class and within a gender-stratified society.

Gachathi Report (1976)

The Gachathi Report (1976) was the second policy document devoted solely to education after independence. It was realized within the economic, political, and social context defined by the 1974–1978

Development Plan. The Gachathi Report emphasized the need for educational changes not only to cope with the sluggish economy but also to stimulate its growth. The report was produced by a committee of twenty-four commissioners, headed by the permanent secretary of the ministry of education, Peter Gachathi. Two of the commissioners were women; one was a headmistress of the oldest African girls' high school and the other a lecturer in the Home Economics Department at Kenyatta University College. The male commissioners included high-ranking academics, heads of postsecondary institutions, senior civil servants, and successful businessmen.

The commissioners solicited background papers from a select group of academicians and educators. Of the thirty-two papers presented, only two came from female academicians, with no doctorates or any significant political or social clout. Invited also for interviews and/or to submit memorandums were representatives of organizations, departments, and interested individuals. The commissioners examined the impact of Ominde's educational policies on the economy with a mandate of providing new directions for education in Kenya to stimulate economic growth.

For a decade since the Ominde Report, Kenya's economy had not grown as anticipated. Instead, unemployment and rural-urban migration rates were higher. The transition from a "traditional" society dependent on agricultural subsistence to a modern society had produced undesirable results that had become impediments to economic growth. School enrollments had been accompanied by high dropout rates. The academic system of education was accused of promulgating the myth that formal education automatically led to high-wage employment in the modern urbanized sector of the economy. This myth had resulted in heavy rural-urban migration in search of nonexistent jobs (Gachathi, 1976, p. xvii). The commissioners claimed that school leavers (graduates) did not have the skills that were required in major areas of national development (Gachathi, 1976). Education had, however, successfully provided some highly skilled labor for participation in the modern sector as well as for Africanization.

Although it was perceived that the education system had performed poorly in its role in national development, the commissioners recommended new policy directions to be adopted so that education could play its rightful role in national development (Gachathi, 1976). The Gachathi Report focused on women and education, and education and rural development as areas that could contribute to economic development.

The report pointed out that, although half of the human resources required for national development consisted of women, the general status of education and the skills of women had lagged behind that of men. It noted that if *national development* was to be maximized the *basic knowledge and skills* possessed by women should at least be equal to those of men. The report recommended that "basic educational and skill attributes acquired by women be continually supplemented by lifelong and effective non-formal learning since women are also *biologically responsible for bearing and rearing children*" (Gachathi, 1976, p. 47, italics added).

These policy recommendations aimed at addressing gender disparities in educational opportunities in Kenya that had not been addressed by the Ominde Report. The Gachathi Report noted that the underlying reasons for gender imbalances in opportunities were traditions, beliefs, and prejudices held by people regarding the roles and occupations of women. The commissioners noted that these had to be modified or abolished. Women did not have adequate formal education and the majority of educated women chose careers that restricted them to gender-specific careers such as nursing, secretarial, and teaching. In addition, the Gachathi Report pointed out that:

It must be remembered that the prominent life pattern for the majority of women, even for those who have had good education and training will include essential family responsibilities and in terms of careers, this would mean a life of multiple roles and occasional disturbances. (P. 45)

The report suggested the following policy recommendations to address gender imbalances and to increase women's educational and economic opportunities:

    a. make more secondary schools coeducational (to give more girls opportunities in the larger number of boys'-only schools);

    b. increase opportunities for girls in science;

    c. provide compensatory enrollments for women at the postsecondary and university levels of education;

    d. increase nonformal education and training for women, with particular emphasis on their economic roles;

e. evolve an integrated structure of nonformal education and training at national and local levels and to give emphasis to the role of women in the economy by recruiting more of them as agricultural and extension officers;

f. improve the career guidance program in schools, especially for girls. (P. 47)

The Gachathi Report also recommended the provision of "free" universal basic education for enhancing the efforts toward the equality of economic opportunities and national unity in the country. It stated that the primary level of education would help all citizens contribute fully to social and economic development. Nevertheless, within this "free" education rhetoric, parents had to meet the costs of uniforms, building funds, equipment levies, and activity fee (Gachathi, 1976). The latter costs constitute one of the principal impediment to girls' education and are responsible for high dropout rates among primary and secondary schoolgirls.

The Gachathi Report focused on rural areas as sites of development. The report defined development as the totality of the processes of change aimed at enhancing the quality of life of the people living in rural areas. Although policies relating to rural areas are important to women since they constitute 70–80% of the rural populations, this is not the reason why the report focused on rural areas. Rather, the shift from urban to rural development was an attempt to reduce the rural-urban exodus of young, predominantly male, job-seekers, in search of scarce employment.

The Gachathi Report's policy recommendations attempted to break the "official silence" on gender inequities in educational opportunities. It also drew attention to the multiplicity of roles that women engage in as workers, mothers, and/or wives. The report provided an opportunity for the construction of gender as a category of analysis of educational opportunities. Nevertheless, few subsequent policy documents have used gender as a category in the formulation of educational and development policies.

Mackay Report (1981)

The Mackay Report was produced in 1981 by a working party appointed to review the higher education system in Kenya in relation to rural development objectives and to recommend how a proposed second university could better assist in their attainment. This party was appointed by the president of Kenya. It consisted of seventeen men, the majority of whom had high academic achievements. They were all high-ranking Kenyan civil servants, except the Canadian chairperson, Dr. Mackay.

The country was faced with growing unemployment, intensified by rural-urban migration of school leavers in search of limited employment opportunities in the formal employment sector. The role of the second university would be to train individuals with skills to enhance rural development. In addition, the creation of a second public university would enable the government to maintain its control over higher education, which was being threatened by the mushrooming of private universities cashing in on the high number of qualified school leavers, faced not only with lack of access to the local university and university colleges, but who are unable to find jobs or create their own. The private universities' curricula were regarded as not being in line with national planning.

The report recommended the restructuring of the education system from 7-4-2-3 (seven years of primary, four secondary, two advanced level, and three years of university) to 8-4-4 (eight years of primary, four secondary, and four years of university). Each level would be terminal. The report recommended that all students in the secondary level of education needed to take *science and mathematics for graduation.* It also recommended curricula changes at both primary and secondary levels with more emphasis on practical courses to provide skills for self-employment. These recommendations were seen as solutions to the growing demand for higher education, unemployment, rural-urban migration, and a sluggish economy.

This working party did not use gender as a category in its examination of education. Its recommendations were based on twelve topics that they felt encompassed the different areas in need of investigation. None of these topics addressed or raised any issue in relation with women. Nevertheless, the recommendations had a direct bearing on women's participation in education and in economic activities.

At the primary level, the report emphasized practical or vocational courses for self-employment. These included masonry, carpentry, and tailoring. Females were limited to tailoring since masonry and carpentry are traditional male trades. At the secondary level, the report recommended science and mathematics subjects to be made compulsory. This would privilege boys whose schools are well equipped to teach science subjects. At the higher level, the emphasis was on the production of "skilled and high-level manpower" for rural development. The commissioners emphasized scientific and technical skills at the higher level. These are skills that most women do not have the opportunity to acquire because many do not study the prerequisite pure science courses in the lower levels of education. Consequently, these recommendations, though outwardly gender neutral, exacerbated gender inequities in access to educational and economic opportunities.

Wanjigi Report (1982–1983)

The Wanjigi Report (1982–1983) was produced by a committee appointed by the president to examine the unemployment problem with respect to the rural and urban formal and informal employment sectors. This committee consisted of nine men. It was chaired by Maina Wanjigi who was also the permanent secretary in the Ministry of Planning and Economic Development. One member was an academic and the rest were high-ranking civil servants. The report concluded that, "despite the impressive achievements in improving the living standards of Kenyans since independence, incomes were still low and [the] majority of the people were still very poor" (Wanjigi, 1982–1983, p. v). The academic-oriented education system was seen as the major contributing factor to unemployment. The Wanjigi's Report endorsed the Mackay Report recommendations to restructure the education system from a 7-4-2-3 to 8-4-4 system of education and to create a second public university. The report noted that within the 8-4-4 education system, there would be an emphasis on practical skill development and a deliberate exposure to practical problems of the nation (p. 51).

Again, poor economic growth, high unemployment rates, rural-urban migration, expansion in education, and increasing costs of public education were the major factors that influenced policy recommendations. Expansion in schooling meant an increased number of school leavers. "Education and training was costing Kenya 41 per cent of the Gross Domestic Product, making it the largest budgetary allocation to a single government service" (p. 47).

Education was still seen as a tool for solving social, economic, and political problems facing Kenya. The report recommended that the education system by made flexible, relevant, adaptive, and vocational-contrary to the operating one, which was said to be weak, inflexible, and geared toward white-collar jobs despite earlier reports emphasizing vocationalization and rural development. The operating system of education was accused of not adjusting to the changing aspirations of individual Kenyans and to the needs of the labor market in terms of new skills, new technologies, and proper attitudes toward work. The commissioners claimed that this characteristic of the education system had resulted in the "paradoxical situation where acute shortages of manpower and massive unemployment exist side by side" (p. 48).

The Wanjigi Report claimed that existing problems, increasing numbers of school leavers, rural to urban migration, job selectivity, dominance of an academic orientation, and problems in personality development, could be solved by an education that emphasized training for self-employment. Education, thus, was to be manipulated to achieve these goals. Prevocational subjects were to be introduced to make primary level education terminal to provide its graduates with skills necessary for self-employment. The report continued the emphasis on vocationalism and suggested that carpentry, metalwork, masonry, home science, basket making, tailoring, and bookkeeping be introduced at the primary level.

The Wanjigi Report recommended the removal of the distinction between economic and noneconomic activities in relation to women's work in the rural areas since most women were economically active as they contributed most of the labor required for the cultivation of food and cash crops on family holdings. The report noted that

The vast majority of Kenyan women, some 88 per cent of the total, reside in the rural areas and most of them are economically active. . . . Even when women are not busy with economic activities, they are occupied in household duties, which also contribute to the living standards of the household. . . . Usual estimates of female participation rate in the labor force are thus misleading so far as rural Kenya is concerned. (P. 32)

The report also claimed that, although the majority of women in the formal employment sector worked as casuals, more women were participating in the broader occupational groups of professionals, executive, and managerial personnel. The Wanjigi Report observed that:

With a high population growth rate, increasing scarcity of land for cultivation, growing migration of women to urban areas and rising rates of participation of women in educational system, the percentage of unemployed in the modern sector jobseekers has been higher among women than among men. (P. 33)

The Wanjigi Report, however, did not recommend ways to ensure that women were not discriminated in the labor market. The report recommended the introduction of sex education in primary school and primary teachers' curricula since uncontrolled population growth was seen as a major obstacle to economic growth. It justified the introduction of sex education at the primary level on the grounds that "children reached puberty at this stage" and "lack of knowledge about sex and reproduction has been one of the causes of pregnancies among school girls" (p. 57). Nevertheless, the report failed to address the victimization of adolescent girls whose pregnancy marks the end of formal education. The report also did not address the issue of the men who are responsible for these pregnancies who, most of the time are teachers or other mature men. These men often threaten and coerce the girls into engaging in sexual activities and then disown the girls when they become pregnant.

Kamunge Report (1988)

The Kamunge Report (1988) was the fourth report solely devoted to education. It came four years after the implementation of the 8-4-4 system of education first recommended by the Mackay Report. The Kamunge Report examined the 8-4-4 educational philosophy, policies, and objectives to ensure that they were in consonance with changing social, cultural, economic, and political demands of the country. The 8-4-4 system had been hastily implemented without physical facilities, workshops, teaching, and learning materials. Furthermore, the government could not cope with the financial demands of this system. A working party was appointed to work out an intensive cost-sharing plan for financing education and training in the country. This party consisted of eighteen commissioners two of whom were women. Most of the men were senior civil servants. One of these women served as a secretary. The chair of the working party was James Kamunge, the director of education.

The report emphasized the centrality of education and training in helping the nation to meet the many challenges of socioeconomic development. It stressed the need for education and training to offer the youth skills and attitudes that lead to self-reliance, self-employment, and prepare for life and employment in the rural areas (Kamunge Report, p. 1, emphasis added). The report noted that although education was a vehicle for economic development, the government of Kenya could not afford to finance the expanding education system. Kenya was under pressure from the World Bank and from the IMF to reduce her educational expenditure that the World Bank and the IMF claimed had contributed to the increasing debt deficit and that was an obstacle to economic development. The World Bank and the IMF proposed increased cost sharing between the government and communities, parents, and beneficiaries of education and training. The working party recommended the immediate implementation of the revised cost-sharing strategy, first implemented after the 1974–1978 Development Plan. The party claimed that the increased cost sharing would "accelerate the expansion of education and training opportunities and thereby increase access to education and training at all levels and to ensure their quality and relevance" (p. 2).

The report did not address gender issues in its examination of the economic problems facing Kenya. However recommended policies such as the increased cost-sharing strategy would have an adverse effect on women's education. The strategy meant that in rural areas, for example, communities would be expected to take more responsibility in the building of schools and teachers' houses. Parents had to cover the costs of books, uniforms, exercise books, activity fees, medical care, and additional fees that the community may impose from time to time. The increasing demand for physical and material labor in order to meet these costs has increased rural women's total work load.

1989–1993 Development Plan

The 1989–1993 Development Plan set the political and economic context for the Ndegwa Report. The plan pioneered the incorporation of the structural adjustment process. It provided policy guidelines to enhance economic growth, and to address unemployment, population, growth, and rural-urban migration. The plan was prepared by the Ministry of Planning and National Development.

The plan attempted to formulate policies that would promote renewed and rapid economic growth, increase productivity in agriculture, raise rural incomes, and restructure industries. In this plan, the general status of women and their role in development was highlighted. The gender discourse on development was in consonance with that in the World Bank Country Study of 1989, which examined the role of women in economic development in Kenya. Contrary to the rhetoric on women's contribution to development, the plan emphasized heavy investment in agriculture in the large-scale but not in the small-scale sector where most of the rural women operate and earn income to afford their children educational opportunities.

Girls and boys' enrollment parity at the primary level was claimed to be a measure of the government's commitment to providing them with equal educational opportunities. This parity, however, was accompanied by a 60% dropout rate for girls that the government attributed to "social and biological" factors (1989–1993 Development Plan, p. 20). These "social and biological" factors were not identified and therefore no policies were recommended to address them.

In the plan, it was noted that most women did not have the education required to participate in the formal employment sector. Most women were concentrated in the "traditional sector where they made a vital contribution in the production of food and cash crops, raising of livestock and provision of essential domestic services" (1989–1993 Development Plan, p. 28). It was pointed out that women have been slow to rise to prominent leadership positions in modern Kenya because of *unfavorable social attitudes*. The low status of women in Kenya was associated with colonialism. The plan claimed that "colonial subjugation and its attendant *Victorian* attitudes toward women both as workers and partners in life eroded women's economic and social status" (1989–1993 Development Plan, p. 28, italics added). The planners claimed that Kenya, however, had been working toward the restoration of women to their active role, not only in the development of the economy but also in the ownership and control of wealth arising from economic production. It was claimed that women's quality of life as measured by such indicators as education, health, urbanization, employment, and incomes had improved considerably since independence. The plan, however, did not substantiate these "unfavorable social attitudes" that limited women from leadership positions. Consequently, these attitudes remained invisible, and incapable of policy solutions.

Ndegwa Report (1991)

The Ndegwa Report (1991) was produced by the Presidential Committee on Employment to address the increasing unemployment, rural-urban migration, and high population growth. The Gulf crisis and a serious external debt burden had made it impossible for Kenya to invest in the economy to improve conditions at home. The committee, appointed by the president in April 1990, consisted of sixteen members most of whom were senior civil servants. Two of the members of this committee were women with impressive academic credentials. Both of these women are advocates of women's rights at local and international levels. The chairperson was Philip Ndegwa who was a permanent secretary. The committee associated unemployment with Kenya's historical colonial legacy of dichotomizing the economy and labor market into urban and rural sectors, formal and informal sectors, and large- and small-scale sectors with a major urban bias.

The tone of the report, particularly in relation to women and development, was in line with Kenya's 1989 World Bank Country Study's recommendations. The report endorsed the World Bank's recommendations such as the emphasis on basic education for women in order to enhance fertility control. The financial support for this project provided by the United Nations Development Program also had an effect on the report.

The report emphasized the role of basic education for economic growth and recommended the provision of universal primary education by the year 2001. It claimed that farmers and informal sector workers with primary education are on-third more productive than workers who have not had basic education, and that educated and literate people are likely to be more productive and will do better in most activities. The report claimed that the education of women "contributes significantly towards many other desirable objectives such as that of reducing population growth" (Ndegwa Report, p. 161). The report drew attention to the high levels of illiteracy rates in Kenya, 44% for males and 57% for females.

The report commended women's economic activities in the informal sector as well as their reproductive labor. It noted women's role in agriculture, food production, cash crop production, and in small-scale industries. The Ndegwa Report also noted women's nurturing roles as mothers and as custodians of family health and welfare, especially that of young children, as contributing to the quality of the country's labor force. It claimed that their *contribution to development* has been *widely acknowledged* in official policy statements and development literature. In addition, the Ndegwa Report alleged that "the government has directed significant efforts at measures for promoting women's development and in redressing the disadvantages suffered by women during *colonial period especially due to the neglect of their education*" (p. 229, italics added).

The report claimed that female representation in the modern sector had risen to over 21% in 1990 compared to 12.2% in 1964. Most of the women in the formal sector, however, were employed in low ranks and were concentrated in the service sector. The report recommended an increase in number of places for women in key positions in the formal employment sector.

The report recommended the following deliberate measures to be instituted by the government to improve women's performance, enhance their productivity and efficiency, and increase their employment opportunities:

1. development planning to be done with specific reference to gender issues;

2. government to implement the Convention on the Elimination of All Forms of Discrimination Against Women;

3. the introduction of a common curriculum for girls and boys in technical training to encourage girls to take up courses that given them more options and opportunities for employment;

4. a policy to increase the number of opportunities for women in key positions in both private and public sectors;

5. women, especially in the rural areas be ensured access to information of importance to them. (Pp. 232–233)

The report recommended that the government increase women's earning potential by supporting them through home-based income-generating activities such as tailoring and food processing, activities that were particularly suited to women's multiple roles.

The report also recommended further increases in parents' contribution to their children's education irrespective of the fact that by 1991 many parents could not meet their current 70% share. This increase has had serious implications for girls' educational opportunities particularly when a family cannot raise its quota. In such situations, a family will choose to educate a boy for cultural reasons. Many girls have been denied educational opportunities on these grounds.

Overall, the report attempted to treat gender issues in Kenya in some detail and made recommendations that aimed at addressing some gender inequities. The inclusion of gender issues in this report could be associated with participants in the committee, and the development discourse of the time propagated by development agencies such as the World Bank and reflected in Kenya's development plans, particularly the 1989–1993 Development Plan. Participating in the committee were two high-level female academics who were strong advocates of gender equity.

Conclusion

In conclusion, I briefly examine the changes in the policy themes and the treatment of gender in the policy discourse articulated in policy documents.

An examination of the public discourse on education shows that since independence, the education system has undergone a series of changes and restructuring aimed at enhancing social, economic, and political development. Economic growth and politics have played a central role in determining the direction of education.

At independence, the Kenya government was faced with two major problems that education was assigned the responsibility of solving. The first and more immediate was the need to provide competent Kenyans who could take over from the departing colonial administrators. The second and more challenging was the long-term problem of devising a system of education that would address itself to the complex political, social, and economic needs of an emergent nation (Wanjigi Report, 1982).

At independence, education was called upon to enhance the rights of all citizens unhindered by the consideration of race, ethnicity, and religion. It was to provide the Africans with high-level skills and access to professions and senior positions in banking, industry, and into all significant activities of the modern world that had been beyond the reach of Africans before independence (Ominde, 1964). Important at this period was the racial factor. The African/race variable, therefore assumed a "genderless" Kenya where opportunities had supposedly previously been limited by race only.

The Ominde Report also recommended the provision of free basic education for all. At this historical point, education was perceived as a right of every Kenyan. This view of education changed in subsequent policy documents, for example, the Sessional Paper # 10 noted that education was more of an economic than a social service. It noted that economic growth was the guiding principle upon which all policies in independent Kenya would be made and implemented. The paper warned that free education could not be provided at the expense of economic growth. The 1974–1978 Development Plan went further and pointed out that education was not a right but a privilege and a scarce item. It recommended the implementation of the cost-sharing strategy to reduce government spending on education. From this time henceforth, Kenyans were compelled to take more responsibility for educating themselves. Subsequent policy documents such as the Kamunge Report and the Ndegwa Report recommended increased cost sharing where parents would have to meet over 80% of the cost of education. These policy changes attempted to devise a system of education capable of addressing itself to the changing social, economic, and political needs of the country at specific historical points. Other educational policy changes have included shifts from an emphasis on academic education to vocational education, employment to self-employment, and urban to rural development.

The Ominde Report inherently emphasized academic education for white-collar jobs in the formal employment sector. A decade later, the 1974–1978 Development Plan noted that the formal sector could no longer absorb all the school leavers. the country was faced with poor economic growth, a high unemployment rate, and rural-urban migration problems that were linked to the academic system of education (Wanjigi Report, 1982). This led to the recommendation of restructuring the entire education system from 7-4-2-3 to 8-4-4 with each level being terminal. The new system of education was to emphasize the vocationalization of school subjects to offer graduates at every level, skills for self-employment and for rural development (Mackay Report, 1981; Wanjigi Report, 1983; Kamunge Report, 1988; Ndegwa Report, 1991).

Also, an examination of the policy discourse articulated in the policy documents shows variations in the conceptualization of women's role in national development. Some policy documents paid substantial attention to gender issues and to women's roles in national development while others did not raise gender issues. The introduction of gender issues in the policy discourse was influenced by the focus of the policy document and by other factors including the prevailing development discourse orchestrated by development agencies and the gender representation in the committees and working parties. Of importance is the nature of gender issues that were raised and how they were framed. Some documents emphasized the role of women as economic and political agents in the public sphere. They emphasized the need for women to have equal access to higher education and scientific skills to participate in the formal sector. Others emphasized women's reproductive and productive roles in the private sphere and recommended that they be offered basic education and nonformal education that enhanced their delivery of these services.

The Gachathi Report paid a substantial attention to gender issues. This report noted that while women constituted over 50% of the human resource required for national development their education lagged behind that of men. The report recommended policies that would not only increase women's participation in higher education but also in scientific and other traditionally male-dominated areas. The Gachathi Report conceptualized women as economic agents in the public sphere. The report recommended policies that would ensure that women become active participants in all levels of the formal sector.

The Gachathi Report policy outcomes could have been influenced by the United Nations Declaration of 1975–1985 as the women's decade and by the participation in the committee of Joan Waithaka, who was the principal of Alliance Girls High School, the first African girls' high school in Kenya. This school has established its reputation as a center of academic excellence. Kardam (1991) argues that individual actors can affect change.

The 1989–1993 Development Plan and the Ndegwa Report conceded that women were underrepresented in the formal employment sector and specifically in positions of power. The 1989–1993 Development Plan blamed this underrepresentation of women in the formal employment sector and specifically in positions of power on prevailing unfavorable social attitudes linked to "colonial subjugation and its attendant Victorian attitudes toward women both as workers and partners in life" (p. 28). Although colonialism has had its negative impact on women's economic and political power, precapitalists' gendered assumptions continue to be used to deny women social, economic, and political opportunities in postcolonial Kenya. The Ndegwa Report, however, called upon the government to implement the Convention on the Elimination of All Forms of Discrimination Against Women. In addition, the report called for a deliberate policy to be put in place to increase the number of women in key positions both in the private and public sector. Implementation and enforcement of these policies would have significant changes in the modern sector and in the general Kenya society.

Beginning in the late 1970s, policy makers began to focus on rural areas as sites of development. Even though women constitute over 70% of the rural population, the focus on rural areas was not based on their needs. This focus became necessary because the country was faced with poor economic growth, unemployment, and rural-urban migration of predominantly male job seekers. Thus, the Gachathi Report recommended policies to improve living conditions in the rural areas and to make them attractive to live in.

This report linked rural poverty with a lack of knowledge, skills, and resources. The report recommended the improvement of the pattern of distribution of incomes and pricing structures in the rural areas as a way to reduce the rural-urban migration. The Wanjigi Report and the Ndegwa Report focused on rural women's productive roles. The Ndegwa Report "praised" women for the laborious unpaid domestic work they perform as mothers and wives. They defined women's work to include food production, petty trading, childrearing, care of the sick, the aged, and a multiplicity of other activities that women have to undertake to sustain their families' welfare. The Wanjigi Report argued that women's labor in the private sphere contributed substantially to the economic development of the nation, and it should be classified as "economic" rather than as "noneconomic" as it had been previously defined.

The Ndegwa Report and the 1989–1993 Development Plan commended women's reproductive labor and its contribution to national development. The Ndegwa Report argued that the country's labor force depended on women's performance as mothers; as custodians of family, health, and welfare, especially that of young children. The Gachathi Report recommended that women's basic education and skills be supplemented by lifelong and effective nonformal education since women were *"biologically responsible for bearing and rearing children"* (p. 47, italics added). However, women's sexuality was inherently blamed for the high rate of population growth, which was identified as a factor contributing to the low economic growth experienced in Kenya. The Ndegwa Report recommended that women be given basic education as a way of controlling family size since there was evidence that the willingness to use contraceptives increased with education. The implication of these recommendations is that rural families and women in particular have become the target of family-planning programs. The policy recommendations on population growth and women's participation in education and in the economy—particularly in the informal sector—were in line with development agencies' policies on development in Third World countries. Although the policy discourse articulated women's reproductive and productive roles—particularly in the private sphere—the policy discourse did not underscore the gender-related factors that have limited the women's agency in both private and public spheres of Kenyan society.

80

TABLE 5.1 Policy Reports: Summary

Name	Year	Overall Purpose	Treatment of Gender
Ominde Report	1964	Review existing system of education and advise the government on the formulation and implementation of new national policies for education.	Recommended girls-only secondary schools. Rejected appeals for girls-only boarding primary schools.
Sessional Paper # 10	1965	Elaborate on the principles of a democratic African Socialist State as per KANU Manifesto declaration. Economic growth as the guiding principle upon which all policies in independent Kenya would be made and implemented.	No discussion on gender issues.
1974–1978 Development Plan	1974	Planning for enhancement of national development within the context of internal and external crisis. Cost sharing introduced.	No discussion on gender issues.
Gachathi Report	1976	Examination of the impact of education on the economy with a mandate of providing new directions for education to stimulate economic growth.	Substantial attention to women's education. Recommended policies to address gender imbalances and increase women's educational and economic opportunities.
Mackay Report	1981	Review higher education system in relation to rural development. Restructuring of the education system from 7-4-2-3 to 8-4-4. Each level would be terminal.	No discussion on gender issues.
Wanjigi Report	1982–1983	Examination of the unemployment problem with respect to the formal and informal sectors in both rural and urban contexts.	Addressed women's economic activities both in the urban and in rural contexts. Recommended introduction of sex education in schools.
Kamunge Report	1988	Recommend ways in which education and training may offer the youth skills that lead to self-reliance and self-employment. Work out a cost-sharing plan for financing education and training.	No discussion on gender issues.

(continues)

(Table 5.1 continued)

Name	Year	Overall Purpose	Treatment of Gender
1989–1993 Development Plan	1989	Pioneer incorporation of the structural adjustment process. Provide policy guidelines to enhance economic growth, to address the problem of unemployment and population growth.	Commended women's economic activities growth particularly those women living in the rural areas. Reiterated government's commitment to the provision of equal educational opportunities to both boys and girls. Low status of women in the formal employment sector was associated with colonialism.
Ndegwa Report	1991	Committee appointed to map out strategies to deal with the increasing unemployment, rural-urban migration, and population growth.	Commended women's economic activities in the formal and informal sectors. Recommended policies to enhance women's reproductive and productive roles.

6

Kilome Women's Educational Experiences

I left school in Standard 3 (grade 3) because there was no school fees for me. There was no money to educate me and they [parents] did not know the usefulness of educating a woman.

—Interview, July 1994

I was asked to perform most of the roles that a grown woman performed and also the work that my brothers should have been doing but they were not at home to do their work.

—Interview, July 1994

I n this chapter I examine Kilome women's educational experiences and those of their daughters. As these excerpts indicate, for most women, their fathers who controlled and allocated economic resources in their families, favored the education of boys rather than that of girls. The women's stories reveal that some fathers did not invest in the education of girls because they did not consider Western formal education important for their daughters at that time. These fathers could afford to educate all their children but only chose to educate their sons. For other women, their fathers' choice of who was to be educated became necessary when they were faced with the lack of economic resources. At these times, fathers chose to invest in the education of their sons for economic and cultural reasons. The women were forced to leave school and eventually get married to establish their "own homes." Marriage was the only option available to them.

First, I discuss the colonial legacy of education in Kenya. Present-day gender inequities in formal education can be traced to the colonial policies on education in which formal education was developed along gender and racial lines. Next, I discuss the women's experiences of education. Their experiences show that gender was used as a criterion in the provision of educational opportunities. Consequently the women were denied educational opportunities equal to those of their male counterparts. Next is a discussion about the educational experiences of the daughters of Kilome women. The girls' experiences are told by their mothers and also by some of the girls themselves. These experiences give a glimpse of the gender factors that continue to limit girls' access to educational opportunities in contemporary Kenya. The women's narratives show that women in Kenya do not enjoy educational opportunities equal to those of their male counterparts. Mothers in contemporary Kenya, however, are aware of the importance of women's education and they have become intervention agents for their daughters' education unlike mothers of the previous generation.

Colonial Background

Traditionally, gender divisions of labor were relatively clear. Men cleared the land and prepared it for planting, looked after cattle, went hunting, and fought in tribal wars. Women concentrated on household chores, cultivated the plots that men cleared, and planted and harvested food crops (Sifuna, 1990). Women also "were full participants in the economy beyond the household and played significant roles in the political decision-making process" (Staudt, 1987, p. 189). Women had more equitable access to resources than they did under colonialism, and parallel female and male authority structures often helped to protect women's interests. Certain traditions and practices protected women and their children, for example, in my culture, a man could not take on another wife without the permission of his first wife and the clan. It was the first wife who picked her cowife. This tradition maintained the first wife's position of power and control of family resources. Growing up in a "modern" polygamous home where my father did not adhere to the traditional rules governing marriage I saw my mother stripped of the power to control the family resources.

The coming of the Europeans and the onset of colonialism dismantled precapitalist gender roles. Men were given a semiformal education to prepare them for work in settlers' farms and in the lowest echelons of the colonial administration. On the other hand, women were left in the rural areas in charge of all the household work. Men were prepared for entry into the world of paid work while women were left in the villages to provide unpaid work to subsidize men's poor wages.

Colonial policies were detrimental; they discriminated systematically against women in limiting access to such new critical resources as Western education and wage labor (Robertson & Berger, 1986; Stamp, 1989). Attempts by women to participate in the formal employment sectors, particularly in the urban centers, were not encouraged by the colonial administration. In addition, Obbo (1980) argues that "lovers and husbands positively resented the employment of women because it brought them in contact with other men and afforded them some degree of economic independence" (p. 10). The consequence of this has been the translation of precolonial gender divisions of labor into relations of domination and exploitation of women (Freeman, 1988). The colonial legacy of women's exclusion from formal education and from the employment sector has continued in independent Kenya.

Kilome women attest to the continued preferential treatment of boys in being accorded educational opportunities. The women's discourse on education show that cultural beliefs about femininity limited their formal educational opportunities. This became evident in our discussions on the education of women. The women talked to me about their views of girls' education, whether it is necessary to educate girls and to what level. Then I brought the issue of women's education closer to them by talking about the education of their own children and in particular their daughters. We discussed the constraints and possibilities they face in their attempts to afford their children educational opportunities and how these experiences are related to their past educational experiences and to their access to economic opportunities. Finally, we talked about the women's formal education, exploring what shaped their experiences and why.[1] I present the women's own experiences of education in the following section.

Women's Own Experiences of Education

A preference for sons in according educational opportunities is one factor that forced some Kilome women to leave school. This gender divide in the provision of educational opportunities is centered around the cultural assumptions and meanings associated with being male or female as defined and shaped in precolonial, colonial, and postcolonial Kenya. The interplay between the cultural definitions of women, in particular the belief that girls will get married and leave their family and the fact that parents have to invest in their children's education, has limited girls' educational opportunities. In most families, girls continue to be viewed as temporary members of the family and as potential mothers capable of "terminating" their schooling to pick up their more "significant" roles of being mothers and/or wives.

Many women from all the sites, Kyandue, Kithumba, and Salama, noted that they had to leave school because their parents, particularly fathers, did not believe in educating women. What hurt some of the women most is the fact that their brothers could go to school for as long as they desired. This was not a choice given to the women. I will be quoting my conversations with the women extensively. This gives the women the opportunity to speak to the readers. In addition, the reader gets the opportunity to reconstruct his or her meanings and understandings of the women's lived experiences. This process makes multiple analyses of the conversations possible.

I use MN to denote the voice of the researcher and the first two letters of the women's pseudonyms. Ngina, whose conversation is quoted in the opening of this chapter had the following to say about her experiences of education:

> Ng: I left school in Standard 3 because there was no school fees for me. There was no money to educate me and they [parents] did not know the usefulness of educating a woman like me and I believe if they knew how useful education is, they would have struggled to educate me. . . . The boys continued with their schooling and left school in Standard 6 voluntarily to go and work.
>
> MN: So there was no money when it came to investing in the girls' education?
>
> Ng: Yes it becomes harder to educate girls but for a boy, it seems as though the money to pay for their education somehow is made available. (Interview, July 1994)

Ngina feels that her parents were not aware of the importance of women's formal education. They expected her to do all the female-

related chores performed by grown women. Ngina's parents prepared her for female roles in the private sphere as a mother and
wife to be a child bearer and rearer, food producer, care giver, and
to provide all other labor required to sustain the household. She
was not prepared to take up a major role in providing the economic
resources required to afford her children educational opportunities.

Ngina received little support to get an education in the three
years she went to school. As she notes " The two last years that I
went to school I did it [paid school fees] for myself... just trying
to keep myself in school against all odds *(kwisukumiiia)*." Ngina
had to thrash sisal to sell so that she could buy school supplies.
This was in addition to the many chores she had to do. These were
not only female specific chores but also chores that had been performed by her brothers such as looking after the livestock. Ngina
had the following to say about her work:

Ng: I had lots of work to do. I used to look after the cows,
fetch water, dig, and plant when it rained. So I was asked to
perform most of the roles that a grown woman performed and
also the work that my brothers should have been doing but
they were not at home to do their work. So, I feel that my
parents did not encourage me to get an education. My parents
just wanted me to concentrate on what women do, not to go
to school but work in the *shamba* [plot], collect firewood, fetch
water, grind millet, cook, and a whole lot of things.

MN: Why?

Ng: Because our parents were not educated. I think they used
to believe that... when a girl was born everybody expected
her to get married since she is a "woman." (Interview, July
1994)

The chores that Ngina did were many and demanding. She obvi-
ously did not have time to concentrate on her schoolwork. The
training she got prepared her for marriage not for participation in
the public space.

Women who do not get married and have children outside
wedlock are considered bad role models. Many mothers, like Ngina's
mother, still teach their daughters domestic skills in preparation
for their "own" homes.

Meli, too, left school after one year of formal education in the
mid-1960s. Her father chose to educate her brother instead of her.

Meli, who was about forty-five years of age at the time of my fieldwork enrolled in primary school when she was a mature girl. She left school and stayed at home helping her mother with household chores and later got married. She has seven children, four girls and three boys. She points out that "I only went to Standard 1 and my father did not want to educate my sisters and me. He was a drunkard . . . He only educated our last-born brother who is a teacher now" (Interview, July 1994).

Thirty-three-year-old Janet, a mother of five, was asked to leave school temporarily after nine years of formal education (Form 2)[2] to ease her father's burden of paying school fees for four children in the secondary school level. She was the only one asked to leave school; her three brothers continued with their education. Janet never went back to school. Getting married was the only option that she felt was open to her.

Ja: When I was in Form 2 at the same time I had three brothers in Forms 4, 3, and 1 and my father was carrying a big burden and I was told to stay at home for some time and I will be taken to school later. I sat[3] at home and I never went to school. All my brothers, even the little one who was in Form 1 when I was in Form 2, went up to Form 4 while I was still at home. I stayed home for three years and I decided to have my own home [get married]. . . . What else could I do? I had stayed at home for three years and they didn't seem to want to take me back to school. They did not mention anything to do with my schooling for all those three years I stayed at home. Although I think my father really wanted to see his children educated he drinks too much to care. [laughs]

MN: But he didn't buy alcohol with his sons' school fees!

Ja: Actually he seemed to really want to educate the boys but not us girls because my elder sister had to leave school in Form 3 because of school fees. She later got married. (Interview, July 1994)

Younger women as well as older women were denied educational opportunities due to their parents' preferential treatment of their brothers in according educational opportunities. Mumo and Manduu point out that in the late 1930s and 1940s when they were going to school, most parents did not value women's education. Parents feared that education would "spoil" their daughters since they would leave the village to go to the city to look for paid work. In the late 1930s, those parents who allowed their daughters to go to school only gave them enough education to be able to read and write letters to their migrant husbands.

Mu: I stayed in school for only four years and then I was supposed to go to intermediate school and my father told me that I could not go to the intermediate school which was at Mbooni about fifty kilometers from here. For them, that was too far. He told me that I had already had enough education since I could read and write. My brothers remained in school but only one of them was very good in school. He became an electrical engineer with Power and Lighting. Us girls we were very good in school; my younger sister, especially, was very good. She had such a good brain but she too had to leave school after Standard 4 because my father said that was enough for her. She later got married and died. (Interview, June 1994)

Mumo later told me that if her father would come to life again, he would chase his sons from his land and give it to her because she is the only one who had made something out of her life. Her brothers, she noted were a disgrace to her father.

Manduu who is about fifty-two years old was discouraged from continuing with formal education by her parents. She was withdrawn from school to stay at home and to help her mother with domestic chores as she awaited a suitor. Her brothers were encouraged to continue their formal education with the father paying the small amount of fees that was required at that time.

Ma: I only had one year of schooling and I left school. I had a very good mind because within one year I learnt how to read and write in Kikamba and now I know how to read Swahili. I had to leave school and after a short time I got married.[4] My brothers did not have to leave school as I did. They went up to Standard 6 (grade 6) of those days and were able to look for work in the city. For them it was OK but all this is because parents those days did not know the importance of a woman's education as we know today. Parents those days believed that girls who got educated got spoilt because they would go to the cities to look for employment like men. They believed that their daughter would become a prostitute; she would be out of sight and beyond her parents' control. And when she decided to get married, she would marry a stranger. Parents of those days wanted their daughters to be married to their friends' sons who would pay bridewealth. (Interview, July 1994)

Some women mentioned that they got their education because their mothers intervened for them. Mwelu, who is forty years old and a mother of seven, had four years of education against her father's wish. She is the only literate woman in her family. Her mother looked after the cattle, a task assigned to Mwelu since her brothers had entered formal schooling. Mwelu stayed in school for as long as her mother could afford to pay her fees. Mwelu left school at the beginning of the intermediate level (grade 5) when her mother could no longer afford to pay her fees. Mwelu had the following to say:

> Mw: I went to school when I was a big girl and I left four years later. My going to school was like a mistake because my father never used to educate girls and he had said that he would never educate girls. Up to that level, I was educated by my mother. I was supposed to look after the cattle because in my family, *girls were the ones who looked after the cattle* (italics added). I was the first of the girls to get some formal education. In my mother's house, I am the only girl who knows how to read and write *[kwiyiandikia]* and we are a family of five girls and two boys. The others never went to school. I went to school as though I was hiding *[niilye oouu ta niivithite]*. My father harassed my mother a lot for letting me go to school and her looking after the cows when I was at school. (Interview, July 7, 1994, emphasis added)

Traditionally, among the Kamba people, boys looked after the livestock. However, with the introduction of formal education along gender lines, more boys enrolled in schools and these traditional tasks were assumed by girls and women thereby increasing their total work load.

Mwelu's brothers were given the opportunity to get a formal education to the levels they desired. They have been able to get paid employment and in turn to support their families and to educate their children. Mwelu's opportunities to enter into paid employment were significantly limited by her lack of educational opportunities. Nevertheless, she needs to earn money to feed, clothe, and educate her children. The survival of her family is dependent on her ability to create income opportunities for herself since her husband has a limited income and is a heavy drinker.

Maria, the most educated rural woman that I interviewed, had thirteen years of formal education and was educated by her mother. Her father made it clear to her that he would not invest in her education but was prepared to educate his sons. Maria's father, however, paid the sons' school fees until her mother objected to his marriage to a second wife.

Ma: My mother paid my school fees because my father said that he would not or never educate girls. That's how I got an education. But in 1981 my father stopped paying school fees for my brothers because he disagreed with my mother. My mother had to go to work in a coffee plantation one hundred and fifty kilometers away in order to pay my brothers' and my school fees. I am the only one who got advanced level education in my family. (Interview, July 1994)

Postcolonial fathers continued to deny their daughters educational opportunities even though they had evidence that the education of women was important. Three young women, Nduki, Mbeti, and Kambua from Salama town left school after sitting for their secondary school entry examinations because their fathers refused to pay their secondary-level school fees. These women were denied education not because of the scarcity of resources, but because the fathers did not value the education of women sufficiently to invest in it. Unlike in the 1930s in the case of Mumo and in the 1950s for Manduu when most parents thought education would have a negative impact on women, Nduki and Mbeti left school in the 1970s and Kambua in the early 1990s. They stayed at home helping their mothers with household work until they left home to look for paid employment in Salama and to get married.

Two of these women, now both about thirty-five years old, had seven years of primary education in the previous 7-4-2-3 system of education and the other one aged nineteen had eight years of primary education in the current 8-4-4 system of education. All three women noted that they left school because their fathers simply refused to pay their school fees. These women's mothers had no resources with which to pay for the education of their daughters. Nduki, one of the women, got married but separated from her husband about ten years ago. She has built a house for her two sons and herself in her father's compound. Her father does not want her in his compound and her brothers worry about sharing the little piece of land with their nephews. Nduki is struggling to buy her own land—a venture that is almost impossible because she does not have a source of regular income. Nduki's sisters face the same bleak future because the father has refused to pay school fees for the girls. Nduki notes the following:

> Nd: When he told me that he was not going to educate me, I was really confused and I saw that there wasn't any other life for me. My mother too was so much under his control; she had no voice and she couldn't say anything. My mother is one of those women who cannot discuss anything with her husband. In the first place my father is a very harsh man and even when my mother suggests anything to him, he doesn't listen to her. Anyway, I stayed there [home] for a short time and I went to work as a house girl. I was very young, just fifteen years. I was not of age and I had not planned to get married but I got married anyway but our marriage did not last very long. He neglected us [herself and her son] and so I had to get help from my parents' house. (Interview, September 1994)

Mbeti tells a similar story of her father's refusal to educate her.

> Mb: I went to school and left in Standard 7 not because my father couldn't afford to educate us but he just did not want to educate girls and that has always shocked me. My mother couldn't manage to pay my fees as there was also another girl in school. So I left school and I stayed at home for a long time and I saw the number of problems just increase beyond what we could bear. My father was not supporting us, neither was he supporting my mother and so I decided to go and work and help my mother and I left to come and work for her [mother]. I have educated those who were behind me [younger]. Some have gotten their Form 4 education. . . . I saved money and took some dressmaking courses. I continued to work very hard after this and I am now self-employed. I have rented a sewing machine and I am a seamstress and that is how I earn the money to support my mother, brothers, and sisters. (Interview, July 1994)

Mbeti is single and has no children of her own. She has worked very hard to give her siblings the educational opportunities that she was denied by her father. She left home and went to look for work to assist her mother to educate her siblings. Mbeti's mother could not leave her home to go and work outside the home because she is responsible for the day-to-day running of the household. Her mother is responsible for all household chores, childrearing, caring for the sick and old, food production, and raising animals—a multitude of responsibilities that demand her full-time attention. These responsibilities limit a woman's participation in the income-earning activities outside the home.

The youngest participant, Kambua, left school because her father did not want to pay the higher fees charged in secondary schools. She has taken the only job available to her—that of a barmaid. She received eight years of formal education and wanted to get a secondary education like her brothers. However, Kambua was asked by her father and elder brother to repeat Standard 7 even though she had passed Standard 8 and had been admitted into a local secondary school. Kambua's father, who holds a well-paying job with a government corporation, had chosen to invest in the education of his sons. Kambua's mother could not intervene for her because she has no access to income-generating opportunities.

The stories of these women reveal patriarchal control over women's education as well as the critical role that mothers play in the education of their children. The inability of these women's mothers to intervene in their education has limited their educational opportunities and has left them with very few economic opportunities, for instance, Kambua works as a barmaid. This is a job that she never thought she would be doing but picked it out of desperation. When Kambua was in school, she hoped to complete her secondary level of schooling like her brothers and train as a nurse or a teacher. These professions require at least twelve years of formal education with passing grades in mathematics and a science subject, biology or chemistry. Kambua's story illustrates her dilemma.

> Ka: I took this job because it was the only job that I could find. I was desperate and I needed money. It was hard to accept to work as a barmaid. You know it is not a good job; it is bad because sometimes our patrons say horrible things to us. They call us men "trappers." The women who live and work here in Salama are not good either; those women who are not working as barmaids feel that they are doing better jobs than us . . . like those who have [a] small business. They too call us "prostitutes." The men too are bad. When they see you there in the bar they think that you are there for them [to prostitute]. They don't respect us at all, they call us prostitutes. I just persevere these insults because I know that I am not a prostitute and this is not what I really wanted to do.

I wanted to train as a teacher or a nurse after my fourth form. I thought it was nice for me to become a nurse or a teacher. I had no intentions of leaving school but you see what hurt me is that they wanted me to repeat Standard 7 not even 8 in another primary school that is so far from my home. I thought that was being cruel. They had no reason to ask me to repeat. (Interview, September 1994)

Even though Kambua's goal was to become a nurse or a teacher, training opportunities were limited by qualifications and space. Her chances of ever being considered for these professions were reduced to nothing when she was denied a secondary-level education. Nevertheless, Kambua hopes to quit working as a barmaid to get married and have her "own home."

Kambua's mother was not in a position to speak for her daughter. Her son's views on the future of Kambua were more valued by her husband—a very traditional view where women are considered inferior to the male children. Kambua noted her mother's lack of power. "She, she had no power to speak on this issue. My father is the one who works and decides how the money is to be used" (Interview, September 1994).

The severe economic crisis that Africa is facing has had an extremely detrimental impact on education (Mbilinyi, 1998) and specifically in the education of women as illustrated by the experiences of the women of Kilome.

Educational Experiences of Kilome Women's Daughters

Recent statistics on education show that the enrollment rates of girls in Kenya, particularly at the primary level, are approaching parity with those of boys. In 1991, girls constituted 48.7% of the total enrollment, a gender ratio that has remained constant since 1989. However, a large number of girls who enroll in Standard 1[5] drop out of school before they reach Standard 8, the last year of this level. Fewer girls move onto the secondary level of education. The high drop out rates among girls are indicative of the existence of gender-related barriers that steer more girls than boys out of the education system. It is important to note that national statistics tend to mask regional disparities.

From the women's stories, it becomes clear that gender has continued to be used as a criterion for the provision of educational opportunities. Men and fathers, particularly in the case of these women, have the economic power from employment or inheritance (property and land) and make decisions on who is to be educated. Their decisions are influenced by gendered cultural assumptions, competition for scarce resources, and the perceived value of women's education.

Women noted that most men do not appreciate the value of women's education in the modern environment. Janet was concerned about her daughter who was in Standard 6 and who was going to be sitting for the secondary entry examinations in two years. Janet's husband, a primary schoolteacher, had already indicated that their daughter would not receive a secondary-level education but would be taken to a vocational school to learn dressmaking skills. Janet felt that her daughter's employment and income opportunities will be substantially limited if she left school in Standard 8. She wanted her daughter to receive a secondary-level education because it opened up more educational and economic opportunities. Janet had no paid employment, but she was working on ways to accumulate finances that would afford her daughter a secondary level of education. Janet had the following to say about her husband:

> Ja: I really don't understand the way men are. You know how they can be. You can't really tell what he is up to and I have been trying to stress to him [husband] the importance of giving our daughter a chance to go to secondary school but he doesn't want to listen to me. So I decided to plant a lot of French beans and sold them and saved all the money secretly *[ngilitye ki]*. I then used this money to start a small business. I sell maize meal in a kiosk. I am working very hard for my daughter's sake, otherwise she will not see the inside of a secondary school because my husband does not want to pay for her secondary education. It is hard to understand why he is refusing to educate her but I will do my best. I don't want my daughter to go through what I went through. (Interview, July 1994)

Janet, however, needed more than finances to provide her daughter with the education that she deemed meaningful. Janet was being forced to make a choice between disobeying her husband and educating her daughter—a choice that could jeopardize her marriage. Nevertheless, Janet was working hard to save money to accord her daughter educational opportunities denied her by her father for being a woman.

The neglect of girls' education was pervasive. Twenty-eight-year-old Kavuli from Kyandue village, too, was concerned about her daughters' education. She had four children, all of them girls. The husband had not paid school fees for them and he had not bought the required textbooks. The two girls, aged six and eight had been sent away from school. Kavuli's husband gets angry when she asks him to let her go to talk to her daughters' teachers and does not know what to do anymore. Kavuli has no money to buy books because her husband stopped her from continuing with her hair-braiding business that was her only avenue for making her "own money to do my own things." Kavuli's other hope was to get money from the women's group revolving credit program. She planned to take any action necessary to get her daughters in school. Kavuli's anger was understandable because she too was a victim; in a remote rural school she aced her secondary entry examinations, and was admitted to one of the best girls-only schools in Kenya but never went because of school fees.

Ndele too told of how her husband had never prepared to give their daughter a secondary-level education. Without Ndele's initiatives, her daughter would not have sat for her university entry examinations in December 1994.

Nd: I started making traditional baskets when I took my daughter to secondary school. When she entered Form 1 had a lot of problems *[thina mwingi muno]*. I used to be told by teachers that my daughter is very good in school and therefore I should look for money to take her to secondary school. They knew that she would pass her secondary entry examinations. When I would tell my daughter's father what the teachers were saying about her, he would tell me not to panic; he will educate her. I advised him to start saving . . . because I have been told that the child is good at school. He would assure me that there will be no problem when the time comes. The problem came when my daughter did her examinations to go to secondary school. The father lost his job; this was about four years since I had started asking him to save money to educate her. So I started wondering what to do with this child; the father is not working and she was called to Kasikeu secondary school. I wondered what to do because I did not have any money and the father had saved nothing. He hadn't saved anything not even a cent! . . . I felt very poor in my heart and I wondered what this child will do being the *first born and a girl and I did not want her to get married as I did* (italics added). Then, I just put a lot of effort and tried the best I could to get her to school. This is about four years ago and surely he does not know how I manage to pay her school fees. Can you imagine what would have happened to my daughter? (Interview, July 3, 1994)

The interviews with the high school girls attest to the crucial role that mothers were playing in the education of their children. Ndele's daughter noted that without her mother's hard work, she would probably be employed as a house girl or would be married. Ndele's daughter talks about her mother's role in her education.

Ja: My mother has been paying my fees. It has been very hard for her to pay my fees and to look after the family without much help from my father. She raises some of my fees by fetching water for the school. She wakes up very early in morning to go to the well to fetch the water. Also she makes baskets and sells them. That is how she manages to keep me in school. Without her I would not have come this far and so I am working very hard to pass my university entrance examinations. (Interview, June 1994)

Women in Kilome division are concerned about men's indifference toward the education of girls. They have realized that the education of their daughters depends on the mothers' ability to contribute the physical and material labor demands associated with schooling.

Conclusion

The women's stories show that women in Kenya do not enjoy educational opportunities equal to those of their male counterparts. Fathers who have continued to be the principle "breadwinners" in the household control the allocation of resources and have tended to invest more in the education of their sons than that of their daughters. Gender has continued to play an important role in determining who is given time and resources to get educational skills and thus participate in economic roles in the public sphere.

These stories show that sons were provided with the resources that they required to access educational and economic opportunities, while the girls were forced to assume roles that were their brothers' in a precolonial context. The choice on who was to be educated was based on gendered cultural assumptions about femininity and masculinity. Girls were seen as potential mothers with the major responsibility of childbearing and childrearing. The sons were seen as future heads of households, breadwinners, and bearers of the family name. The women left school and helped their mothers with the household chores and eventually decided to have their "own homes." Getting married was the only viable option for most of these women. Two younger women, however, chose to find any available paid work to help their mothers. As Ahlberg-Maina (1991) observes, gender is an important category along which power, property, prestige, and social regulation are organized, regulated, distributed, and given meanings in a gender-stratified society. Stromquist (1987) also observes that cultural norms and division of labor within the home limit girls' educational opportunities, being defined primarily as future mothers. She further argues that these cultural norms are not challenged in schools; instead, they are reinforced.

In addition to cultural norms, poverty and famine continue to limit girls' educational opportunities in Kilome and in many other parts of Kenya. In many schools in dry areas, boys greatly outnumber girls particularly in Standards 7 and 8 (grades 7 and 8). During famine, girls are the first victims of food shortage as they are forced to drop out of school to marry or to seek employment. In Kilome, like in most other areas, girls tend to mature while in the lower classes. This is because most girls start school late and they tend to be retained more because of poor school attendance resulting in poor achievement. In addition, parents request their daughters to be retained in the primary levels particularly if they have other children, especially sons, in the secondary level. This eases their financial pressure. As one headmaster observed, "a girl who is 15 and still in Standard Six (grade 6) will not resist the pressure to get married. The bride price is still a popular way of getting the much needed cash and property" (Mbataru, 1999).

The increasing severe economic, political, and ideological crisis that defines Africa has had an extremely detrimental impact on education and has undermined efforts to equalize educational opportunities (Mbilinyi, 1998). The debt crisis has forced governments to reduce public expenditure in education and in other social services. Women and girls are the first victims of these structural adjustment policies.

Nevertheless, we see that mothers are taking an active role in the education of their children, and daughters in particular. They have become crucial intervention agents for their daughters in the provision of educational opportunities. As Cubbins (1991) observes, women's economic power has a positive influence in the education of both girls and boys.

7

Factors Limiting Girls' Educational Opportunities

I think the beliefs that existed [a] long time ago are still lingering with us.

—Interview, 1994

This chapter discusses the factors that women identified as limiting girls' schooling in Kilome division, Kenya. The women's discourse on education shows that gendered cultural assumptions about femininity are invoked to deny women/ girls educational opportunities equal to those of their male counterparts in contemporary Kenya. They identified traditional preference to educate sons, assumption that girls will get married, and girls' potential motherhood as the gendered cultural assumptions that limit girls' schooling. The rising cost of education has exacerbated gender inequities in the provision of educational opportunities in Kenya and has become a major barrier to girls' education. Pervasive poverty among many rural households delineates the circumstances upon which decisions on whose education is worth investing in are made. The women's articulation of the factors that impede girls' educational opportunities is matched by their determination to challenge these barriers and to afford their daughters educational opportunities denied them by their fathers because of social, cultural, and economic factors.

I first discuss the high cost of education followed by a discussion on son preference and girls' marriage and potential motherhood.

Next is a discussion on responsibility for sex education. Finally, I discuss poverty in rural areas.

High Cost of Education

The high cost of education, particularly at the secondary level, has become a major limitation to children and in particular, girls' educational opportunities in Kilome division and in Kenya today. The government has reduced its spending on education as part of its implementation of the structural adjustment programs imposed by the IMF and by the World Bank. Parents have to invest more in the education of their children through the cost-sharing strategy, and school fees have skyrocketed. Besides paying school fees, parents have to purchase textbooks, stationery, mattresses, bedding, cutlery, and many more items depending on the school. Previously, the government provided most of these requirements. The financial demands have become unattainable for most families who rely on a single income or who have no income at all. For a long time, men have been the only income earners in a family. However, this study shows that the financial demands on each household are way above the incomes from most wage employment. Consequently, women and mothers have had to engage in a multiplicity of activities to increase the family's income to meet, and barely so, the financial needs of their families.

The challenges that women face as they attempt to educate their children are enormous. In addition to limited resources, mothers are further impeded by the number of children they have and by the cost of educating them particularly at the secondary level. A mother's determination to educate her children is frustrated when the latter complete their secondary level of education and their certificate/diplomas are withheld by their respective schools because of fee balances, for example, Mulee, a mother of eight, had two daughters whose certificates were withheld because she owed the schools 9,200 Kenya shillings (approximately $135). At the time of the interview, redeeming the certificates was not a priority because Mulee had two other children in secondary schools and they needed money to remain in school. Without the certificates, however, Mulee's daughters are trapped because they need them for entry into the work force or for further training. The withholding of certificates is a problem that has not been documented.

Because of the high cost of schooling, more women have to leave school without the necessary credentials and/or skills to participate in the economic activities in the public sphere. As Wausi and Mutheu, two professional women pointed out, "in Kilome, women's education is worse off than it was ten years ago." With the demand that parents invest more in the education of their children, families are making choices on who is to be educated. Poverty and gendered assumptions about women are influencing parents', particularly fathers' decisions on whose education, a boy or girl's, is worth investing in. Girls are denied educational opportunities and some have been sent to work as child laborers to help feed their families or even to educate their male siblings. As Wausi observed, the situation of women's education in Kilome is pathetic. She associated this situation with poverty.

> Wa: It is a bad thing we are so poor, I think if there was more help from the government in terms of facilities or education . . . these days, kids in school are not supplied with any textbooks in schools. The only thing the government gives to schoolchildren is the free milk. There are no textbooks, exercise books, and pencils. In our time, much as we were poor, we were supplied with textbooks, exercise books, and pencils. If you want to read a book today, you have to buy it. I think now, given the population has increased, I think there are fewer women in the rural areas who are making it than there were those days. I think ten years ago there were more girls making it through the education system than today, particularly from Kilome. It is getting worse; there is a lot of poverty. (Interview, September 1994)

As the women noted, more girls, particularly those living in the rural areas where parents have little or no income-generating opportunities are not getting any meaningful education since the government reduced its spending on education. Kenya has been under IMF surveillance since 1975 and the fund has a permanent monitoring official who oversees government budgetary decisions. The IMF has applied restrictions to social spending: education, health, and welfare services expenditure. Although social spending topped the list in the 1964–1973 decade, it has been at the bottom since then (George, 1994).

     Implementation of the structural adjustment policies (SAPs) imposed by the IMF has had a detrimental impact on education (Mbilinyi, 1998), particularly, the education of women. The government's reduced spending on education has forced parents to invest heavily in their children's education. School fees have become a major issue in many families.

> Mu: These days school fees is an issue. Before, it wasn't such a big issue. It was manageable but now when they [children] get to Form 1 the money involved is quite a lot. These days a parent might be forced to decide who to take to school and who not to. I would say that these days, there is a very high possibility of parents doing that. They are making choices and often they don't favor girls. (Interview, September 1994)

School fees became a major issue with the introduction of the cost-sharing strategy in the early 1980s, which meant less government spending on education and more parental contribution to the education of their children. This strategy was imposed on Kenya by the IMF/World Bank to help the government deal with its deficit which, the World Bank argued, expenditure on education contributed to substantially. Interesting though is the fact that the IMF has never applied its restrictions on military expenditure and costly presidential entourage whose expenditure by 1986 was estimated to be $23 million a year (George, 1994).

There is no definite amount as to how much parents are charged for the education of their children. Official figures of total costs of education show that the preprimary level of school is the least expensive costing 600 Kenya shillings year with the government contributing 2% of that amount. The primary level of education costs 2,100 Kenya shillings ($40) per year with the government contributing 44% of that figure and 7,500 Kenya shillings ($150) per year for secondary level of education with the government contributing 27% of that amount (Ndegwa Report, p. 172).

Although the official costs of education seem affordable, the reality is that the tuition and nontuition fees charged at all levels of education are higher than the official figures quoted. Parents with secondary-level children indicate that fees in secondary schools range from 9,000 to 20,000 Kenya shillings per year ($300–$700) or more. These fees are highest in the first year of secondary school, particularly for those students who, in addition to buying school uniforms, have to buy bedding, a charcoal/paraffin stove, utensils, and other necessary boarding items depending on the school. Capital requirements have become major barriers to children's access to educational opportunities particularly at the secondary level. This situation has forced parents to make choices on who is to be educated and in which school, a harambee day or a government-maintained boarding school. When parents have had to make a choice between investing in the education of a boy or a girl, the choice is clear.

Traditional Preference to Educate Boys

Traditionally in Kenya, sons have tended to be valued more than daughters. Even in these modern times, most monogamous marriages have turned out to be polygymous ones if the first wife has "failed" to bear a son. Son preference in Kenya can be observed right from the moment of birth (Eshiwani, 1983). This attitude seems to influence the educational opportunities that are made available to boys and girls.

Since the introduction and development of formal education in the twentieth century, women's education has lagged behind that of their male counterparts because gender was used by the missionaries, colonialists, and the local indigenous people as a criterion for allocating educational and employment opportunities in Kenya. The educational experiences of Kilome women of different ages showed the persistence of son preference in the allocation of resources in the acquisition of educational opportunities. Mulee's experiences of schooling were as follows:

> Mu: I really did not attend school well. . . . I used to be sent home so often and at Standard 7 I left school because my younger brother caught up with me and I was asked to stay at home to let him to be educated. I used to be made to miss school many times and I would be asked to repeat classes; eventually he caught up with me and I was asked to leave school because my parents couldn't afford the school fees. (Interview, July 1994)

Although the introduction of formal education along gender and racial lines has had a negative impact on the education of women, parents' preference to invest in the education of their sons has exacerbated gender inequities in accessing educational opportunities. The fathers' preference to invest in the education of their sons, rather than in the education of their daughters, is influenced by precapitalist beliefs about marriage and family. Among the Akamba, for example, families were and still are patrilineal and family descent is still traced through the male side. Property is still acquired through inheritance and it is only sons who can inherit property as well as the responsibility of the family in the father's old age or when he dies (Muthiani, 1973). Similarly, in the modern context, education is viewed as an inheritance to be acquired by the ones who will take the family's responsibility and carry on the family name. Therefore, if a family disposes of its property such as livestock and land to educate a son, he is expected to take responsibility of the family and to look after his aged parents when he finally enters the formal employment sector.

Assumption That Girls Will Get Married

Among many African peoples, marriage is seen as a focus of existence, a duty, a requirement of the corporate society, and a rhythm of life in which everyone is required to participate (Mbiti, 1990). A Muûkamba family continues to be patrilocally extended and women leave their homes to go and establish "their own homes" at their spouses' homes.

The interplay between high monetary costs of education and the potential of adolescent girls to become mothers limits educational opportunities made available to girls. Many rural families with non- or limited income-generating opportunities are forced to sell their property, usually land and livestock, to educate their children, particularly at the secondary level of education. Women from Kilome division noted that very few men dispose of their property, especially land, to educate girls because of the gendered cultural assumptions about womanhood.

Traditionally land belonged to the clan or family but not to individuals. Land was used communally and was not considered a property to be inherited like livestock. However, the land registration policy introduced by the colonial administration and reinforced by postcolonial land policies stipulated that land be registered in the name of the head of the household who was assumed to be the man. Under this policy, a man in whose name the land is registered owns the land and controls the products of that land. He is the only one entitled to make decisions on the land. Land has become a very valuable property that has increased its value with the population boom. It has become a scarce commodity and a source of serious family disputes. Payment of secondary school fees is one of the few reasons why a family would consider selling a piece of land. Most men, however, will not dispose of their land to educate girls since they are considered "transient" members of the family. It is assumed that when girls mature, they will get married and leave their families. Most fathers feel that investing in a daughter's education is an unwise move, a precarious venture because she may become pregnant and leave school and/or she may get married and leave her family and her education will benefit her husband's family that did not invest in her education.

As Ngina observed, many fathers feel that it is not worth investing heavily in a daughter's education.

Ng: I think the same beliefs that existed long time ago are still lingering with us. When a man educates his daughter, he feels that she will take that profit [*vaita*] to somebody else's home. Some people still feel that if they educate their daughters, they will leave and get married. That is not true. (Interview, July 1994)

Kilome women noted that some girls' educational opportunities are limited because they are expected to get married.

Me: I feel that girls do not stay on in education because many parents argue that they shouldn't spend money educating girls because they will get married but these days there isn't a girl and boy. All children are the same and, if the one who you see has an interest and puts effort in school, you should educate that one without discriminating. All children are the same and any child who is interested in education and works hard should be encouraged and supported by all means. (Interview, July 1994)

The gender discrepancies in investing in the education of girls and boys are widespread and women from all the sites reiterated that it was extremely hard for men to dispose of their land to educate a girl. The women agreed that:

It is very hard for men to sell their land to educate girls. They wouldn't agree. If there are any they are very few and we have not heard of one. They [men] will sell land and cows to educate sons. [women in a chorus] Men can sell all the cows and leave the barn empty to educate their sons. (Kithumba women's self-help group, July 1994)

Therefore, the increasingly high cost of education is limiting girls' educational opportunities particularly at the secondary level. Because of the physical and material demands of the education system, parents dispose of their property (land and cows) to educate their children. There is still a strong belief that a woman, no matter how much education she gets, will eventually get married and move out of her home and take all that education to benefit her spouse's family. The question that the parents ask is: What happens if the family disposes of their land to educate their daughter who, after acquiring the education and a good job, gets married and leaves the family, or worse still, she drops out of school because of pregnancy? Women, however, note that gender relationships in marriage change to the benefit of the woman if she is educated. Ngina observed that:

> Ng: If your daughter has an education, she does not have to get married. If she does get married, she doesn't have to get married in the real traditional meaning *[ti kutwawa ni kutwaana]*; it is no longer getting married but the man and woman marrying each other. My desire is to have my daughters educated more than the boys because they are more empathetic than the sons. If your daughter is not educated and therefore has no job or means of earning her own income, she will have to struggle with her husband to get anything [support] from him to support herself and her parents. (Interview, July 1994)

Culturally, women are expected to get married irrespective of their level of education. The two professional women who participated in this study noted that they had been pressured to get married by their parents and by the society in general. Koki's parents sought suitors for her. The choice to marry, however, was hers.

Whether married or not, women are now expected to support their parents unlike in the traditional setting where sons were the only ones expected to support them. Koki, in fact was expected to pay school fees for her brothers and sisters and to support her parents. She noted that her parents expected more from her than from her brothers and sisters who are working and are married. The parents wanted her to contribute money toward family projects (e.g., land and a new house for the parents) but she knew that she will not inherit any of them. She pointed out that her married sisters were not asked to contribute because the parents argued that those married have their "own homes" to worry about. She wondered why her parents do not understand that she is a single mother and has the sole responsibility of her daughter.

The professional women could resist the pressure to get married because they did not live in the village in their parents' homes. They did not have to ask for land to support their children. These women have well-paying jobs in the city and they do not experience the pressure that their rural counterparts experiences. As Wausi noted, even though she would like a partner, she shouldn't be rushed to find one. Finding one is her choice. Akamba culture expects all girls to ultimately get married and have their own "homes." Muthiani (1973) points out that a home, as the Akamba saw it, is a family that is comprised of parents and their offspring or the nuclear family. A home also included grandchildren. It is therefore understandable why women who are not married and have children are not considered as having "homes." The cultural expectation that girls' should ultimately become wives and mothers has become an impediment to girls' education.

Girls' Potential Motherhood

In Kilome division there is an increase in the number of girls leaving school because of pregnancies, particularly at the senior primary and secondary levels of education. Kilome women identified this as one of the reasons why men are hesitant to invest in the education of girls. Girls who get pregnant in school are expelled from school with little possibility for reentry into the formal education system. Girls are doubly victimized as a result of pregnancy. When a girl leaves school because of pregnancy, the repercussions of her deed could be far-reaching. In extreme cases, fathers might refuse to educate the other female children and to blame the mother for her daughter's "bad behavior." Mwelu described the situation quite eloquently.

Mw: There are many girls dropping out of school due to pregnancy even though it seems that nowadays girls have learned other ways of avoiding pregnancy. There have been very many such that out of forty girls in a class, about twenty leave school because of pregnancy. Those who "persevere" to the end are quite few, not many. That is one form of failure. If one gets a child while in school, that ends their education because one cannot be a mother and a student at the same time. You cannot manage both. For others, their fathers are very angry when their daughters get pregnant and feel like sending the daughters and their mothers out of the home. Others refuse to educate daughters who come after the one who left school because of pregnancy. Some parents stop paying fees for all their daughters because of one girl's mistake because they do not want to waste their money. That's it. If a daughter gives birth, she disheartens her parents. Some parents as I said refuse to pay school fees for all the other daughters and maybe this daughter was not going to have a baby like her sister since all children cannot be the same. Some parents fail to understand their daughters because some girls who give birth don't do so willingly. Sometimes they don't really know what they are doing when they get involved with the boys. (Interview, July 1994)

Mothers whose daughters have children outside marriage or drop out of school because of pregnancy tend to loose the respect of the community. One mother, Mariya, had two daughters who left school because of pregnancy. These girls were not able to reenter the school system. The pregnancy of the two girls is seen as a threat to the mother's ability to bring up her daughters appropriately. It is not surprising that Mariya found it difficult to talk about her daughters' reasons for their dropping out of school. My conversation with Mariya went as follows:

MN: Are any of your children in secondary school?

Ma: I have 10 children. The first two left school before they completed secondary level, they were *defeated* and they are married now.

MN: What do you mean by "they were defeated"?

Ma: Why, they were defeated by school means that they went through the wrong path.

MN: Meaning what? I really don't understand what you are saying!

Ma: They got pregnant and because of this they couldn't go back to school. (Interview, July 1994, italics added)

Nzula, a friend of Mariya, felt that she had to answer this question for Mariya. She had the following to say:

Nz: You see . . . let me answer that one for her . . . that is the story we were telling you . . . that is how it happens. Now you a woman [mother] you want to educate this girl, you want to take her back to school and your husband tells you that "because your daughter gave birth, she can not be taken to school" and you have no money. So what do you do, tell me? (Interview, July 1994)

Mariya was embarrassed to talk about her daughters' pregnancies. Her feelings are understandable because, when a daughter has a baby outside wedlock, the mother is blamed for not having taught her daughter acceptable behavior including the fact that illegitimate children are not welcome in the homestead. Often, the father directs his anger at the mother and at the daughter and, in many occasions, the father asks the girl to leave the homestead. The lucky ones get married to their babies' fathers; others have no where to go and stay home where they are treated with hostility. Pregnancy tends to mark the end of formal education for the girls involved irrespective of whether the girl gets married or not. Investing in a girls' education is therefore considered a risky business.

The women of Kilome felt that girls still seem to value marriage more than education. Maria noted that "while the community expects women to get married, the girls are not resisting this culture and seem to jump at any opportunity to get married. They value marriage more than a job." It is very rare to meet a woman who was never married. Although roles within marriage have changed with time, there is still that strong message sent to girls that when they are of age, they should get married and have their own "homes." A single woman is considered incomplete. Besides getting education from schools, mothers try to give their daughters skills related to motherhood and wifehood. Women who leave their husbands because of abuses are still pressured to go back to them. Maria, who had the most number of years of formal education and who was living in the rural areas has been pressured to go back to her emotionally and physically abusive husband. She has resisted this pressure and was determined to use her father's land and to support her children. Maria's situation was unique because her mother had passed away and her father had deserted the family leaving them a productive piece of land that Maria and her two brothers had agreed to share. Maria did not want to go back to her husband or to get married to anybody else. She noted that "when a woman gets married, she is trapped and it becomes impossible to reenter the education system (particularly if she hadn't completed secondary school) or search for paid employment." Many men, the women noted, did not want their wives to work in the city. The assumption that women will become promiscuous if they work outside the home limits their participation to activities in the private sphere.

Responsibility for Sex Education

Unwanted pregnancy is one of the factors that limits girls' educational opportunities. However, as Wausi, one of the professional women, pointed out, there was no one educating girls about their sexuality. Traditionally, grandmothers discussed sexuality issues with their granddaughters. However, youngsters learned about sex in the traditional dances that they attended. The coming of the missionaries marked the end of these traditions that were perceived as evil. To Wausi, Christianity or religion has become a major barrier to the possibility of addressing sexuality issues. She noted:

> Wa: I think the biggest problem is this *witikilo* or "Christianity," I keep telling you about. People avoid the whole issue of talking about sex and yet it is responsible for a lot of the problems. I mean so many girls drop out of school when they are in primary and in secondary school because of pregnancy . . . you just hear so and so's daughter is pregnant; people want to avoid issues like telling their daughters that you can get pregnant; they also want to avoid issues like telling her that "you know, if you really must do this you better do abc" and of course there is also the other moral from the Bible like "you are single; you should not be having sex." I mean, like I found that when I got to college, suddenly you are in a relationship and you can't even make a decision about getting contraceptives because there is a part of your mind that tells you, "God, the minute you do that you will start saying yes to every man and you are just as good as a prostitute." And I think that happens a lot in common; it is like here you are into something and every other person is doing it and yet you know a lot of them are in very stable relationships but you can't just bring yourself to make that decision . . . [there are] a lot of moral issues that a lot of us have not sorted out by the time we get to college or even whatever time we become sexually active, yet. Parents do not want to admit that their daughters are sexually active.

There is some denial also and . . . that the good girls are the ones who get . . . it. Yet there are a lot of good girls who make a small mistake. I think it is an issue that needs to be addressed very cautiously and seriously and have a lot of time devoted to constantly making young people aware of the dangers of . . . and all that it is involved. I don't know. It frightens me about my own daughter. (Interview, September 1994)

Teenage pregnancy is a concern of every parent, particularly mothers who are held responsible for teaching their daughters morals around sexuality and the consequences. As Wausi points out, the issue of sexuality is complex and mothers are not sure how to address it in the modern context. In the precolonial contexts, young people learned acceptable norms through grandmothers and age-group rituals such as circumcision. Mothers are apprehensive of exploring the technological choices for controlling reproduction with their daughters because it would be equivalent to promoting promiscuity. Abstinence is the most preferred method of contraception, but the reality is that most girls are sexually active.

The women noted that they did not discuss sexuality issues with their daughters. All they expected from them is to be "good girls" or "well behaved" to avoid getting pregnant.

Ma: It is true that we parents do not talk about sex with our daughters. We behave as if we are scared of each other and somehow we hope they learn about it in schools or somewhere else; I don't know where. The problem is that we parents are not very close to our daughters. . . . I don't know whether that is the reason but it is just so hard for you as a mother to talk to your daughter about such things. You see, in the early days our grandmothers used to talk to us about what would happen if we slept with boys. (Interview, June 1994)

As Mariya pointed out, mothers need to develop a close relationship with their daughters so that the latter can feel free to discuss their sexuality with them. The dilemma that most parents face is how girls should be told about using contraception without compromising assumed standards of morality. Also, there is concern about whether schools should be teaching girls about sexuality and what should be taught in the classes.

Women and girls are being held solely responsible for childbearing and childrearing. However, it is important that both boys and girls are made aware of the consequences involved so that girls are not doubly victimized for getting pregnant. Of importance too are how girls become sexually active. Often the men involved are adults who coerce the girls into sexual relationships that result in pregnancies. Girls need to be taught about their rights and provided the space to discuss such abuse without being blamed for provoking it.

Poverty

Underlying the gendered cultural assumptions that limit girls' educational opportunities is poverty. In a society created by the colonial administration, which is divided between a comparatively small urban elite and a large impoverished and mostly rural population, families are having to make decisions and choices of who is to be educated based on gender. Women form over 78% of the rural adult population. In these impoverished conditions, women in the neocolonial era have limited access to resources and have little control over resources that the family owns. Women are the poorest of the poor since even poor men have poorer wives and children (Vickers, 1991). Women are, however, well aware of the importance of girls' education and are committed to providing their children with educational opportunities but most women lack the resources or the economic power to afford the high fees charged in schools specifically at the secondary level. Nzula put the dilemma that women face succinctly.

> Nz: If you are told that there is no money to educate your daughter, what can you do to push the child ahead? If my husband comes and says there is no money and I am not working and I have no authority to sell land. . . . You see men are the ones who sell land. I can't even sell land. What can I do? (Interview, July 1994)

Colonial and postcolonial development policies shifted the control of communal land to individual men assumed to be heads of households. The shift has meant that men control the land and its products and that women's access to land is mainly through spouses or male relatives. Market-oriented land policies have had a negative impact on rural poor, the majority of whom are women and their children. As Vickers (1991) argues, the recession, the debt crisis and structural adjustment policies have placed the heaviest burden on poor women, who earn less, own less, and control less. Women care for children, the aged, the sick, the handicapped, and others who cannot look after themselves. They service the household with food, cleanliness, and clothing and in many cases water and fuel. When rains fail and food prices rise and wages fall, a woman must spend more time finding ways to satisfy her family's hunger, often eating less herself in order to feed her husband and children. Women's activities are labor intensive and mostly unpaid.

Women in Kenya have limited sources of income. Female participation, as a proportion of modern wage employment, was 22.1% in 1991 with most of the women concentrated in traditional female domains characterized by low pay, poor working conditions, and no benefits (Republic of Kenya, Women's Bureau/SIDA Project, 1993). Low participation of women in the formal employment sector is a consequence of colonialism. Colonial policies such as the development of a formal employment sector in the urban areas with high-paying jobs for those educated, the need for a semiskilled African cheap male labor, and the provision of education and employment opportunities along gender lines are factors that have limited rural women's participation in activities designated as "significant economic activities." Their concentration in activities designated as "noneconomic" has impeded their struggles to afford their children educational and economic opportunities.

Poverty is pervasive in the rural areas such as Kilome division. As Mutheu observed, poverty and famine have made it almost impossible for parents in this area to afford their children educational opportunities particularly at the secondary level.

Mu: First, families in Kilome have to buy food from the shop, the rains are bad, and we have overpopulated the land. The fact that food has to be bought competes with school fees.... You see our area has a lot of problems. We have very few girls' schools and others go to faraway schools and there are many problems with this too. Bus fare has gone up and you have to buy so many things because these days they go with so many things—bedding, besides soaps and school fees and especially to go to Form 1 if you as a parent want your child to be a bit comfortable, you must have at least 20,000 Kenya shillings [$400] because you have to buy all things including a basin for bathing and there is also a lot of theft. [laughter] In our days we used to lock up things in lockers or in our suitcases. But these days how do you lock up your mattress in a box? [laughter] or your blanket? Your child comes home and tells you that the blanket has been stolen. There are so many problems and the kids have become small criminals [laughter] because those days we just used to have petty thieves but these days you find kids who steal everything and anything. If you open their suitcases [boxes] you find spoons and these days they are just taking the things from you. The reports that are coming out of schools are scary. This is because there is a lot of property—personal property in schools [laughter] in the dormitories and so the risks are higher. All that burden is on the parent because they are the ones who hear these problems first. And these problems can only be solved with money *[mbesa]* not with maize *[mbemba]*. Somebody else had written in the paper that Form ones look like civil servants when they are going to school because they carry a lot of things: mattresses, blankets, basins, stoves, and a lot of money to pay school fees. The parent has to take that child up to the school because thieves and conmen target these children and so the parent has a lot of work. (Interview, September 1994)

Many rural families live in conditions circumscribed by poverty and this has influenced girls' educational opportunities. Women, such as Kamene and Wanza attest to the impact of poverty on their education. Assertions such as the following give a sense of the reality of women's lives. "I left school in Standard 3 because of poverty." "I went up to Standard 4 and left school because of poverty; we lacked resources." "Do you know how much hardships we endure!" "There is a lot of poverty here." "Do you know that it is because of poverty we are so much behind! Everyone wants to educate her children/daughters but if there is no money how can you give them an education?" (Interview, July 1994).

Conclusion

Women identified the high cost of schooling as a major barrier to girls' education. They also identified gendered assumptions that limit the allocation of resources to girls and deny them access to meaningful educational opportunities. Kilome division women, like women in many parts of Kenya do not control the distribution of resources. Fathers minimize their investment in the education of girls on the assumption that girls will get married and will not take the primary responsibility of their families' welfare. The implementation of structural adjustment policies has resulted in a heavier burden on the poor (George, 1994), particularly women and their dependents. Education of women has suffered heavy setbacks.

Women of Kilome are determined to offer their daughters meaningful educational opportunities to enable them to participate in the public sphere as do their male counterparts. These women firmly believe that education opens doors and offers the opportunity to break the poverty cycle. They have taken new roles and challenges of providing their children with education and economic opportunities. In addition, they continue their roles as food producers, cash crop producers, childrearers, care givers, and active participants in women's self-help groups and in other community affairs. Women's labor is also required for the numerous "development projects" that have been initiated by the government and development organizations in the rural areas that Feldman (1983) argues have little potential for improving the living conditions of rural women. However, the women's agency is evident in their articulation of their experiences, those of their children and in their active participation in resisting, restructuring, and/or transforming their society.

8

Intensification of Women's Labor to Educate Their Children and Its Implications

> I have just had to "deny myself" *[kwiiilea vyu]* or self-sacrifice.
> I don't mind getting extremely tired. I work very hard every
> day. I leave my house in the morning and go back to the house
> at 6 P.M. because if I don't do that my children will suffer.
>
> —Interview, 1994

This chapter discusses Kilome women's economic activities and the intensification of their labor as they assume new roles and challenges as intervention agents for their daughters' education in Kenya today. The women strongly believe that education holds the key to a better future and are engaged in a variety of activities to enable their children, and daughters in particular, to acquire the educational opportunities that were denied them because of cultural, social, economic, and political factors. The fervor for education exemplified by the women has its roots in the resistance and fight for equal educational opportunities by Africans in colonial and postcolonial Kenya.

Discussed first is the importance that women attach to educating their daughters. Secondly, I examine the women's inability to depend on husbands for their daughters' education. Next is an examination of the women's income-generating activities and the intensification of their labor to provide opportunities for their children's needs in a gendered economy. Finally, I examine the limitations of women's activities in making educational opportunities available to their daughters and the effects of women's increased labor to their health, to girls' education, and to the welfare of the women's dependents (children, the aged, and the sick). Austere structural adjustment programs combined with social-cultural beliefs about women are great barriers to women's attainment of equal and meaningful educational and economic opportunities in Kenya today.

Importance Women Attach to Educating Daughters

A majority of girls in Kilome division are leaving school without the educational credentials capable of affording them paid employment or dependable income-generating activities. Both in our group and in individual conversations, the women repeatedly linked education with paid work. The women stressed that there are great benefits in educating a girl because education provides an opportunity for women to become economically independent to deal with their children's, parents', and their personal financial problems without having to ask for money from their spouses. The women associated education with modernity, independence, and status (Bloch & Vavrus, 1998). Unlike some development discourse that has emphasized the provision of women with at least four years of primary education so that they can control their reproduction, Kilome women's desires and struggles are for their daughters to get as much education as possible. These women know that in present-day Kenya, there are no employment opportunities for holders of primary school level education. When I asked one group what kind of education they would want for their daughters, the women responded in a chorus:

> We want our daughters to study hard as you did; we want to see them employed with an income and having their own property. We want to see them self-reliant *[meekwatie]*. If you had not been educated would you have been able to assemble us here? (Kithumba Women, July 1, 1994)

The women believed that education would enable their daughters to challenge the institutionalized pattern of gender relations that involves inequalities of power, sexuality, and resource allocation favoring men over women (Scott, 1990). To Kilome women, a good education means self-reliance through employment. With employ-ment, an educated woman can support her mother and her family, own property, and make marriage choices.

Supporting Their Mothers

The women banked on the education of their daughters as an in-vestment from which they would reap benefits when their daugh-ters enter the formal employment sector. They stressed the fact that daughters are more empathetic than boys are and would sup-port their mothers financially. One woman noted: "What I see is that girls are more empathetic and are merciful. Whenever I get something I always feel that I should give her [mother] some of it because of that mercy. Men are not like that" (Interview, July 1994). Also, some women likened education to a fruit that benefits the entire family whether a woman is married or chooses to remain single.

To the women, education seemed like a panacea for the poverty that has trapped them and their children. Their lived experiences, those of their brothers, and the few fortunate women (myself in-cluded) who had received an education were remarkably different. I could make choices; I could support my children and my mother. The only difference between these women and me was the fact that someone had intervened for me. Likewise, the women of Kilome have decided to become intervention agents for their children and for their daughters in particular.

The women cherished the self-reliance that education seems to afford women. Kambua, a barmaid, was certain that education would have opened more doors than bartending in Kenyan bars, where she was seen as a prostitute. She commented:

Ka: Personally it [education] would have been very important. You see if I had gotten an education, I wouldn't be working here. I wanted to become a nurse. Nurses don't suffer the way I suffer here. Nursing is much better. They [nurses] can do things for themselves. (Interview, September 1994)

These women's stories show that parents still believe that educa-tion ensures reasonably well-paid jobs in the public sector, even though the unemployment rates in Kenya are extremely high. These women still believe a secondary or high school education increased their daughters' employment opportunities. Kilome women's stories went on to challenge the assumption that sons are the only ones who should be prepared to support their parents. Traditionally, sons are expected to carry on the family's name and its responsibilities that include ensuring that their aging parents are given adequate care. Mothers no longer think of sons as the only ones who can support them in their old age. They believe that they would benefit more from their daughters' prosperity than from their sons.

Supporting Their Families

Kilome women would have liked to be able to look after their children and to provide them with educational opportunities just like their educated brothers were doing. Some women noted that if they had been given the education their brothers or their husbands had, their children would not lack necessities such as school fees. Seventy-four-year-old Mumo, the oldest participant caused laughter among the women when she stood and said, " If my father would come back to life today, he would chase his sons out of his land and give it all to me." She pointed out that her father wasted his money and resources educating her brothers who had become "useless" to themselves and to the society. Mumo was applauded by the women. Women noted that most men do not take their families as their first priority as do women. As Manduu observed, educating girls is an invaluable investment that warrants even the disposal of land.

> Ma: I have not seen men sell land to educate a girl but they sell land to educate boys. This is not a good way of thinking because even if the girl eventually gets married, when she gets a job she will not forget her parents. Also, she does not have to get married, and more so, even if she gets married, she will help herself and her family with that knowledge you gave her. And that for a woman is a big benefit because a woman will never go and spend her money on alcohol; she will always take it home and support her children.... Her children are her first priority (Interview, July 1994).

Kilome women felt that education has the potential to open many doors for women. The most important option education affords women is the opportunity to participate in the formal employment sector. The women saw how education had enabled men to enter the formal employment sector, while the women's lack of education shut them out of this same sector. Women earned their money the hard way but spent it all on their families, while some men spent their money on individualistic ventures or habits.

The women of Kilome felt obliged to take responsibilities over the welfare of their families. These responsibilities required the women to have reliable sources of income. However, the income-generating activities that the women were engaged in were precarious and they perceived education as capable of affording women, and their daughters in particular, more reliable income opportunities to meet the needs of their families.

Making Marriage Choices

Making the choice of whether or not to get married was an option that the women of Kilome division cherished. The women saw education and its provision of employment as capable of providing girls with the ability to make choices in life, including choosing to get married or to remain single. The women noted that marriage was no longer a solution or an alternative for girls' education. Indeed, Meli, one of the women, pointed out that "marriage these days is problematic. Women cannot expect to be just their husbands' helpers." She noted that women need to enter in a marriage relationship knowing that they could take care of their children. Many mothers were concerned that their daughters were getting married when they were not capable of taking care of their children. Meli was concerned about her daughter who left school in Standard 4 and got married. She pointed out that her daughter was suffering, and that she would not encourage her other daughters to get married. She asserted that marriage was not a solution if the woman could not take care of her children. A reliable income was seen as a prerequisite for a woman's self-reliance. The women noted that education and training opportunities increase employment opportunities for girls, which are crucial to women's economic independence. They wanted their daughters to receive an education and paid jobs because the other income-generating opportunities available in Kilome and in neighboring divisions were not reliable. The women have had to "sacrifice" themselves in order to have some income to educate their daughters and to look after their children. They did not think their daughters would be able to engage in the type of strenuous work they do. Eighteen-year-old Munee, a high school student noted how difficult her mother's work was and she could not see herself doing the same kind of work to support her family. She noted that her mother only rested when she was sick!

Implementation of the structural adjustment programs has translated into low wages for migrant husbands. Women, like Munee's mother have had to involve themselves in multiple income-generating opportunities to maintain their households. Women's work loads have been greatly increased. The stretching of women's time and energies has caused a deterioration in their health and nutrition (WIN News, 1995). Single mothers, however, are the most disadvantaged of all women.

Single mothers living in their father's compounds were under considerable pressure to find a "home" for their children. Kamba culture does not encourage single motherhood. Land use for building and subsistence by the single mother becomes extremely problematic. Nduki, a single mother who lived with her two sons in her father's compound, felt that marriage was not a solution, even though her father wanted her to get married; he made it clear to her that he did not want her living in his compound. Even though she would like to get married, Nduki observed that marriage was no longer a solution because women can no longer rely on their husbands to meet the families' needs. Nduki blamed her father for having denied her a secondary education that would have provided her with a job like her brothers who have found employment with their secondary-level education.

The pressure to get married is not limited to single jobless mothers. Koki and Wausi, two professional women, each aged thirty-six years, also have experienced pressure to get married. Nevertheless, they were not living in their fathers' compounds and did not experience the pressure and desperation that Nduki was undergoing. They were in a position to make choices. If they did not ever get married, they did not have to live in their parents' compounds; they could afford to buy land or a house in the city. Nduki could not afford this option, which would be best for her and her children. Nduki also had another problem—she had sons unlike the professional women who had daughters.

Traditionally, sons need to inherit some land to build their houses. If Nduki could not get married and she could not afford to buy land, where would her sons build their homes? It is not likely that Nduki's brothers would like to share land with their nephews. Balancing the individual's desire to remain single and the cultural expectation to get married was quite a challenge for Kilome women. As Wausi observed:

Wa: The thing is that much as it is very common to be a single parent; it is not exactly accepted. I don't know whether it is because of our religious society, but it is like ideally people should only have kids when they are married so like I can tell you much as I really wanted to have a baby when I did, it hit a big blow to my self-esteem and ego. It is like somehow, initially I couldn't just strike a balance; it's like I had.... I was not completely acceptable. The assumption was that I should get married; anyway I didn't want to get married. (Interview, September 1994)

Single mothers have learned that motherhood is honored only if it is within the marriage institution. Women who become single mothers experience pressure not just from their parents but from their friends, relatives, and the community in general. Koki, a thirty-six-year-old registered nurse, midwife, and mother of one, has been pressured by peers as well as parents to get married. She has been introduced to various men in the hope of her finding a marriage partner. Professional women find that it is difficult to remain a single mother, and they consider ways to compromise. Wausi felt that marriage for her should not mean getting "married to a man" in the traditional sense, but the two getting married to each other. Nevertheless, marriage to her should be permanent because divorce "scars" a woman. She pointed out that many women marry for material, security, and physical support from their husbands and most of them remained in abusive relationships because of their dependence on their spouses. Fortunately for Wausi the good education she had received offered her many other opportunities to increase her income. Wausi noted that she could make choices not only because she had a good education and a good job, but also because she was also empowered. She felt that many women, some who hold good paying jobs, were still being abused by their spouses. Wausi felt that irrespective of educational attainment, Kamba women are socialized to accept positions of inferiority.

Wa: At least now I can make the choices. I think, fine there is that [education] but at the same time I think there is . . . the way we are *socialized* (italics added), I mean there are so many women who, if you like they have good jobs, good education and they are still abused by their husbands because maybe they have threatened the position of the man in the family. It could be a perceived threat and not a real one. I mean that . . . they feel that they should still refer a lot of things to their husbands. You even see women who take their paychecks to their husbands just to give him that upper hand. Women need to realize that it's not just economic power that gives you that *bargaining strength* (italics added). You've also got to realize that you are an individual and you've got to assert yourself. Don't you hear the Kambas say that "so and so is a proud pauper"?[1] (Interview, September 1994, emphasis added)

Economic independence does not necessarily produce a liberated woman. Women need to resist oppressive traditions and patterns of life in addition to being economically independent. Family relations are a clear indication that, even though women are working to support the family economically in the public sphere alongside men, familial hierarchical identities have not waned. Indeed, in Kenya, at the legal level, the rights and duties of each marriage partner, and even the definition of marriage itself, is unclear and often controversial (Stitcher & Parpart, 1988). Whatever the marriage type, a wife has very little actual protection against the main risks she faces: lack of support, lack of child support, and physical abuse. Wausi, however, made it clear that women's rights must be upheld by the women who should live their lives knowing that "a beggar does not have to lose his or her pride and dignity." Consequently, women, no matter how impoverished, should be treated with dignity.

Women's Inability to Depend on Husbands for Daughters' Education

More and more women have had to take charge of their children's, both boys and girls', education because they are de facto heads of households since many men have migrated to the urban areas in search of employment, they are single heads of households, there is not enough money in the household, and there is the issue of men's preference to educate sons.

Many rural women have become de facto heads of households as their husbands have migrated to the cities to seek employment. These men visit the rural areas at most once a month when they receive their monthly pay. The women are left behind with their children and are supposed to meet their children's needs with the little money they receive from their migrant husbands. Women are the ones who enroll their children in the first level of formal schooling. They are the ones who are responsible for the material and physical labor that is demanded in schools. When children are sent home to collect fees or to buy an exercise book, a pencil, or a school uniform, it is the mother they will find at home. It is not possible to rely on migrant husbands' salaries to meet the educational needs of their children. Therefore, mothers' ability to contribute financially to the education of their children, and particularly their daughters is crucial.

Due to changes in the family structure, there is an increasing number of female-headed households. These single women receive no support for their children's education from the government or from their children's fathers. There is no law in Kenya ensuring that single mothers receive support from the fathers of their children. Therefore, single mothers are solely responsible for meeting the basic and educational needs of their children. Single mothers like Kamene know that their children's access to educational opportunities is dependent on the success of their economic activities. As Kamene observed:

Ka: You see me here I am the only one responsible for the education of those four children that I have. They are all looking at me to provide every single thing they need because I am their father and mother. If my business fails, then all those children sink. (Interview, July 1994)

Women from Kilome division pointed out that some men are simply not interested in the education of any of their children, much less that of their daughters. Several women pointed out that some men do not consider their families their first priority; therefore, women have to become intervention agents for their children.

Some women noted that even though their spouses are working, the salaries that these men receive are not enough to meet the needs of their families. Such women include Mulee, who described the situation succinctly.

MN: What about your husband; you said that he is a teacher?

Mu: Yes, a teacher but don't forget that the household needs exceeds what he brings home. We need well over 10,000 Kenya shillings [$200] and he would bring home about 2,000 Kenya shillings [$40] what does it really come to? Schooling for the girls became a struggle for all of them. And the entire lot of them have had difficulties . . . all my children have had to struggle to get an education because of that. (Interview, July 1994)

Real wages have been declining. A study carried out for the Central Organization of Trade Unions showed that between 1981 and 1983, real wages declined by 20%. At the same time, annual defense spending and interest payments on debt increased by 11.7 and 13.7% respectively (George, 1994). In situations where resources are scarce, we find that men, who control economic resources and their distribution, prefer to invest in the education of their sons rather than that of their daughters.

Intensification of Women's Labor

Women from Kilome division are engaged in a multiplicity of activities in an effort to create educational opportunities for their children and to improve the living conditions of their families. They are not only food producers and care givers, but they are also inventors of a variety of ways to provide the ever-needed cash in their families. The women are engaged in income-generating activities as individuals and in groups. They are active as small-hold farmers, domestic workers, waged employees, petty traders, and in women's self-help groups.

The women 's income is crucial to the provision of educational opportunities for children, and particularly for female children. If a woman is not able to take up the challenge and to serve as an intervention agent, it is clear that more and more children and girls in particular will drop out of school ill-equipped to participate in the changing society. Also, as long as educational credentials continue to be used as prerequisites for paid employment and as long as girls continue to leave school without these credentials, the cycle of poverty that has delineated their mothers' lives will be repeated in their lives as well. Mulee has taken up the challenge, but it has increased her burden. Mulee explained her experiences as follows:

Mu: I sell some merchandise in the local market. I go to Nairobi, buy bar soap, paraffin [kerosene], and potatoes and come and sell them. I use the little profit I make to pay my children's school fees slowly by slowly. . . . I go to the market three times a week but only in the afternoons because I have to make sure that I have done all the other work that needs to be done. I have to make sure that my plots are ready for planting when the rains begin; I must take time to weed and harvest. I also water the vegetables; then there is the daily work that must be done. You know a home cannot run without water, firewood; somebody has to cook; you know what women do, don't you? (Interview, July 1994)

The fact that women have picked up new roles and challenges does not free them from their household responsibilities as mothers, wives, food producers, and care givers. Therefore, women have to balance their time between all these roles including participation in politically initiated community development projects where their labor is also required.

All these factors along with the high costs of schooling have forced women to engage in a multiplicity of labor intensive income-generating activities. Kilome women's sources of income include employment, sale of property and farm produce, and "petty" business.

Employment

Employment opportunities in Kilome division are minimal. There are no big farms and plantations in Kilome where women can find employment. A few women have had to do casual work in neighbors' small-holdings in order to meet some of their children's basic and educational needs. The work includes helping with household work, digging, planting, weeding, harvesting, fetching water and firewood, and cutting napier grass for the cows. Work starts at 8:00 A.M. and ends at 1:30 P.M., depending on the season. Ndunge, a casual laborer, has had to engage in multiple income-generating activities in order to educate her children. Unfortunately, Ndunge's activities are extremely limited because of the high costs of secondary education. Ndunge's situation is as follows:

> Nd: I want to educate all my children without any differentia-tion. I really don't look at some as boys and others as girls. What I don't have is the capability to educate them. I really want to educate them, but I am so poor and I don't know how I will be able to pay the secondary-level school fees. Like for those two children who are following each other, one in Stan-dard 6 and the other in 7, I wonder how I will pay their fee with the little money that I earn. I work for 600 Kenya shil-lings [$15] a month and my husband gets about 1,000 Kenya shillings [$20] as a security person at the market. That helps a little. But the fees are a lot. The first term, my son pays around 4800 Kenya shillings [$90] and second term is about

3,900 Kenya shillings [$65] and the third term we pay 900 Kenya shillings [$19]. This is for day school only. He sleeps at home and it is far. And you should not forget that this does not include the uniform. With the uniform, it is a heavy load and I am trying to make the best. I am pushing him through. He is now in Form 2, and he is doing very well. His total fees per year are about 10,000 Kenya shillings [$200]. (Interview, July 1994)

Although Ndunge was working very hard, she knew that her income was not enough to pay for two children's education at the secondary level at the same time. She had made her daughter repeat several classes in the primary level to give her son the opportunity to complete his secondary-level education. Parents prefer to make their children repeat primary level classes because this level is cheaper than the secondary level. Repetition, however, is one factor, that increases girls' dropout rates. At the time I spoke with her, Ndunge's two daughters were going to be sitting for their secondary entry examinations in the following year. She was deeply concerned about her girls' education after their primary level of education and noted that a mother's economic power was important to afford girls educational opportunities.

Ndunge, who left school after sitting for her secondary entrance examinations, knew that Standard 7 education or primary level education offered few economic opportunities. She wanted her daughters to have more reliable income-generating opportunities that become possible through higher formal education. It is difficult to educate children with moneys earned as casual laborers. The salaries are very low, and the work is labor intensive. Unfortunately, even though these women who work in their neighbors' plots go home exhausted, they still have to do similar duties in their homes!

Although Kilome women were struggling very hard to provide their children with educational opportunities, they saw the high school fees that are charged in secondary schools as a major impediment to their efforts. This worried the women immensely. From the women's stories, it was evident that many girls from Kilome would not get a secondary-level education unless there was an outside intervention. However, the possibility of an outside intervention did not exist. Statements such as "I have one daughter in Standard 8 now and the other I made her repeat Standard 6. I don't think I will be able to afford to pay for their education. I feel that I will not be able to get them very far because the fees that are charged in high school are very high" are indicative of the dilemmas and difficulties that mothers are facing in their struggle to give their daughters educational opportunities.

Sale of Property and Farm Produce

Women from Kilome sold farm produce for income. In most communities, women have more control over food products than livestock. Muthiani (1973) points out that among the Akamba, the participants' ethnic group, family property belonged to the family under the direct responsibility of the male head or guardian. With land policies, men were registered as the owners. Women cannot sell land or livestock without the husbands' permission. As one woman observed:

> I have no authority to sell land. You see men are the ones who sell land. I can't even sell land. What can I do? I can't because he . . . "roared like a lion" and said that this is his home and the rule is that as a woman I cannot disobey; how can I? (Interview, July 1994)

Akamba traditions and land policy introduced by colonial administration in the 1950s and reinforced after independence deny women the right to own property and specifically land. Women can only have access to land through male relatives, husbands, and sons. Women who are single heads of households have no independent access to land. Many women find it difficult to become sole owners of property because to own property one needs credit, and women have limited access to credit since they don't have collateral (Republic of Kenya: Women' s Bureau/SIDA Project, 1993). Without land, it becomes difficult for women to keep livestock or to plant enough food for subsistence as well as for market. It is, however, important to point out that only about 17% of Kenya's land is suitable for agriculture, which provides the primary livelihood for about 80% of the population (UNICEF/GOK, 1992).

Land, rather than paid employment matters more to rural women. Women who have access to land, particularly those with relatively larger plots of productive land, plant food crops for their families as well as for sale. Ngina had a relatively large piece of land that had a small stream in the plot and planted a lot of maize and beans, the staple diet of Akamba people, and used the water from the stream to plant vegetables, onions, and tomatoes for sale. In comparison to the other women, Ngina was doing extremely well. She sold the food crops and vegetables to educate and support her eight children, two of whom are in secondary school and two others in training colleges. She nevertheless pointed out that her way of earning an income was very strenuous—it was a "sacrifice" that she had to make in order to provide her children with the educational opportunities that were denied her. Ngina generated income as follows:

MN: How do you get money to pay school fees for your children, clothe them, and so forth?

Ng: Sometimes I might have sold onions and gotten my own 5,000 [$100] *[nitee kitunguu nakwata ngili syakwa itano].* In fact, last season I earned 9,000 [$180] from onions. Sometimes I find that the father to my children [who works in Nairobi] cannot afford to pay all the school fees for the children. There are times when one of the children has no school shoes; I just go and buy these things without his knowledge. I also pay the children's school fees, particularly those in the primary school and the one in the harambee secondary school. He comes and finds that his children have shoes and I have paid school fees and does not know where I got that money from. He knows that I don't engage in any strange business *[ndiendaa soko ili,* "prostitution"]. I have just had to deny myself *[kwiiilea vyu]* or self-sacrifice. I don't mind getting extremely tired. I work very hard every day. I leave my house in the morning and go back to the house at 6 P.M. because if I don't do that my children will suffer. You have to accept to work hard and very hard indeed and when the rains fall you have to agree and accept that you will be in your plot *[shamba]* whether there is rain or no rain. (Interview, July 1995)

Other women also planted vegetables (kale, cabbages, and French beans), tomatoes, and onions for sale. Rarely did the women harvest enough maize and beans for home consumption and for sale. The women's income from the sale of farm produce was limited by the unavailability of arable land, fertilizers, and water shortages. Few women were as privileged with land and water as Ngina from Kyandue village. The river that used to run across many plots in Kithumba village has lost much of its water because of over irrigation, poor farming practices, and a road construction project that dumped silt in the river. None of the women living in Salama sold farm produce from their plots because most of them did not have access to land and water in Salama. Ngina's story supports Agarwal's thesis that "rural women can best improve their lives and those of their children if they own and control arable land" (quoted in Stackhouse, 1995).

Petty Business

All of the women from Salama town were full-time petty traders while some from Kithumba and Kyandue villages worked part-time. Women from the villages took their merchandise to various marketplaces during designated market days. Rural women could not become full-time traders because they were also responsible for all the household chores. They were the ones who tilled the land, planted food and cash crops, cultivated, harvested, took care of the sick, worked in school, and undertook many other domestic chores. They had to be at home daily to make sure that the livestock and poultry came home safely in the evening. Women with young children found it even harder to be petty traders. Their husbands forbade others from going to the market. Rose's husband forbade her from going to the market because he believed that business-women were promiscuous (Interview, July 1994).

The commodities that the women sold included tomatoes, potatoes, cabbages, and bananas. Others sold bar soap and paraffin. Income from these activities was not adequate to meet the educational needs of the children. Some children were constantly being sent home to collect fee balances. Beth, too, noted that her daughters had to leave school because she could not afford to pay their school fees as the entire family depended on the income from her tomato business. Her daughter had left school in Standard 8 and was working as a maid. Beth was quite unhappy because she did not see how her daughter would break out of the poverty cycle into which she was born and raised.

Be: Now we are all looking at the tomatoes *[tusyaitye ala manyaanya]* together with their father and my mind tells me that in all honesty my children will not go beyond Standard 8. My daughter, who had two years of secondary education, is even very lucky. None of the younger ones will be able to go beyond the primary level. Do you know that it is the money problem that is eliminating each one of them out of school? Now if that happens to each one of them, the result is that they don't even have a place of their own. If you have children and all those problems . . . it becomes very hard. Do you hear what I am telling you? (Interview, July 1994)

The women's businesses were not doing well because they did not have capital and access to credit. Women, such as Mulee traded with only 2,000 Kenya shillings [$50], and the profits were used to pay school fees by installments. Her two daughters had not collected their high school diplomas because of the fees they owed.

The women's stories show that women were trying to increase the family's income by every legitimate means possible. Some women had become petty traders to earn money so that they can meet their families' basic and educational needs. However, their income was not adequate to educate their children particularly at the secondary level of education. Most women could not afford to give their daughters an education that offered them choices similar to those offered sons. The women, however, strongly believed in the usefulness of educating their daughters and basically were sacrificing themselves for the sake of their children's education.

Limitations on Women's Efforts to Educate Their Daughters

Women from Kilome wanted to educate their daughters beyond the primary level. They are aware of the fact that primary education no longer guaranteed the credentials for paid employment or for skills for participation in income-generating activities. After all, most of these women received primary level education and they had experienced untold hardships. However, as Mwelu pointed out, the women's limited income opportunities were insufficient to pay the high fees charged at the secondary level. For Mwelu, her daughters will not get a secondary-level education. She noted that she struggles to get the children to Standard 7 by herself. She is responsible for school uniforms, soap, and everything else that the daughters need. "I get so strained of money such that I cannot afford their fees particularly at the secondary level" (Interview, July 1994).

Many women faced the dilemma that Mwelu faced. They worked hard to educate their children up to the primary level but were unable to pay fees in the secondary level of education. Some women, however, were able to educate their daughters' at the secondary level. Others, like Mulee's daughters, had substantial fees balance that had to be cleared before they could be given their transcripts for the university entry examinations. Most parents chose to take their children to the local day schools even though these schools lack the necessary facilities. Mulee's daughter, who was admitted to a government-maintained school in another district ended up in a private/harambee school and she did poorly in her examinations. As Mwikali observed "we are forced to take our children to the local schools because that is what we can afford and also we can make arrangements with the headmaster to pay the fees in installments" (Kithumba Group discussion, July 1994).

The women's efforts are undermined by the cultural, social, economic, and political conditions in Kenya. The implementation of the structural adjustment policies has served to entrench poverty that is central to the experiences of women. The government of Kenya is the main culprit in the perpetuation of poverty since the biggest cause of poverty in Kenya is poor management and corruption coupled with mismanagement and misallocation of the country's resources (Nation Writer, 1999).

Even though the women wanted to give their children and daughters in particular educational opportunities denied them, the demands on women were overwhelming. Their attempts to cope with the physical and monetary demands of their labor also negatively influenced women's health, girls' education, and the welfare of the family.

Women's Health

The increasing intensification of women's work has had a profound impact on their health. Some women who participated in this study were physically ill due to carrying heavy loads to and from faraway marketplaces. Mwelu was suffering from severe lower back and leg pains. She could not carry heavy loads on her back and had excruciating pains when she bent. This was very hard on Mwelu because most of the women's work in the rural areas involves long hours of bending while planting, weeding, and watering vegetables. In addition, Akamba women carry heavy loads on their backs such as water, firewood, maize, and beans. Worse still was the fact that Mwelu could not afford to see a doctor. The following interview excerpt can give us a glimpse of how Mwelu's income-generating activities have combined with her domestic roles to contribute to her present condition. Mwelu's story is as follows:

MN: What have you been doing to support your family?

Mw: I have been selling food stuffs. I have been buying green vegetables, loquats, and bananas. If I cut a green banana bunch and keep it to ripen, I would go to Mavivye [about twenty kilometers away] market, where I used to take the bananas, green vegetables, and other fruits. I would sell all those things and buy food in the market because food is cheaper in that market than in other markets around there. I would go home carrying a lot of food to last us at least a week. I used to come back and work on my plot *[shamba]* the whole of that week since I would have enough food for that week. If there was a "naked" child, and those days clothes were cheap, I would also buy them clothes in the same market and I would come home and work for a week on my shamba until Monday, the market day. I would go back on Monday to go and sell.

Mw: I liked going to Mavivye market because food[2] was cheap. I could buy more food there, enough for a week. That is what I have been doing.

MN: What are you doing now?

Mw: I just work on my shamba because my back and legs have been paining for quite sometime now. I cannot carry anything. Walking is a big problem for me. I cannot walk for a long distance on foot and I cannot bend to work in the shamba anymore.

MN: You used to carry heavy loads?

Mw: Yes, and maybe the pains are related to that. I don't know but I think it could be because I used to go carrying things and I would come back home carrying things. I used to carry a lot of things and the place is very far. The things I used to carry were way over my carrying capacity. Before this I used to work in my plot/shamba and plant vegetables which I would sell. I do not go to the shamba anymore. I can't really do much because of the pains.

MN: How do you make some money now that you don't go to the market anymore?

Mw: I have concentrated on participating in these women's self-help groups. We contribute 30/= or 20/= and so when it is my turn, if one of my children is naked [without clothes], I buy them clothes and whatever else they need, if I can afford it. (Interview, July 1994)

Mwelu pointed out that she could not afford to pay a private practitioner. Ideally, she was supposed to be referred from the district hospital to the Kenyatta national hospital where she could be seen by a specialist at government-subsidized consultation rates. Unfortunately, the government has reduced funding on health services, resulting in very poor working conditions for the doctors, most of whom have subsequently left public hospitals and joined private practice. Mwelu's body was aching but she had no access to medical care. Ngina,[3] from Kyandue, who talked of having "sacrificed" herself for her children's sake, mentioned that she too suffered from lower back pain.

Women in the rural areas are forced to neglect their health as they get engrossed in meeting their families' material and emotional needs. Women will ignore symptoms of sickness because they cannot afford to take time off to see a doctor and because their health is not a priority in the competition for the limited income they earn. Even in times of food shortages, women tend to eat less. Women's poor health serves as a great blow to their dependents as they become unable to perform their roles as food producers, income earners and care givers.

Girls' Education

Women of Kilome division were certainly playing a major role in the education of their children. As Ngina pointed out, "participation of mothers is a crucial factor in the education of their children" (Interview, July 1994). However, as the demand for women's labor increases some women might have to relegate some of their domestic chores to their daughters. This might mean that these girls will miss school to take care of the younger siblings while the mother takes her wares to the market or she works as a casual. Some parents might also withdraw their daughters from school or fail to take them to school and send them to work as domestics to help support the family. Kamene and Wanza, two women who participated in this study, left school in Standard 3 to work as domestics to help feed their families (Interview, July 1994). At the time of the interview, Kamene was struggling to educate her four children with the money she earned from her tomato business. She expressed deep concern at her inability to meet her children's basic needs and educational needs. Many girls have joined the growing number of child laborers. Child labor is still rampant in Kenya, with some working children are as young as six years old. The little money children earn can never compensate for the environmental hazards they face or the lifelong impact on their growth, especially their psychological, emotional, and educational development (Government of Kenya and United Nations Children's Fund, 1992).

Most domestic workers, particularly children, are the most easily exploited of all workers since there are no set salaries for domestics. The salaries to be paid depend on the whims of the employer. Child laborers are likely to be sexually exploited by their employers and others. These encounters lead to teenage pregnancies and continue the perpetuation of female poverty.

Impact on the Welfare of the Family

When a woman is ill, the whole family suffers because of the multiplicity of roles that she performs. The repercussions are phenomenal. In the Ndegwa Report (1991), it is argued that "the quality of a country's labor force is to a large extent dependent on women's performance as mothers, the custodians of family health and welfare, especially that of young children, aged and sick" (p. 229). The illness of a mother limits the educational opportunities of her children and more so of her daughters who are called upon to take up their mother's roles as food producer, childrearer, and care giver. Female children have also become child laborers so that they can earn money to support their siblings.

Because of the multiplicity of women's roles in the family, particularly as food producers, prolonged illness will subject the family to food insecurity. Women, however, have organized themselves in women's self-help groups to support each other in the changing social, economic, and political context of Kenya society.

Conclusion

The women's discourse on education shows their awareness of the importance of the education of women and of their agency in providing educational opportunities to their daughters. The women aspire to give their daughters education that allows them to participate in the public sphere as do their male counterparts. Kilome women know that women are not just "helpers" of men but are active participants in shaping the lives of their children. The women want their daughters to make choices and to own and control property like their male counterparts. They are aware of the barriers that women face in their efforts to attain educational opportunities. Consequently, they have become their daughters' intervention agents.

The women are engaged in a multiplicity of labor-intensive activities in order to earn an income in a gendered economy. Their income-generating activities are limited and their efforts to provide their children with educational opportunities are impeded by the high school fees that are charged, particularly at the secondary level. The implementation of the imposed austerity policies or structural adjustment policies, has meant severe cuts in social welfare expenditure that includes education and health services. These policies have created profound hardship in many poor countries—Kenya included, especially among relatively vulnerable subpopulations such as women and children. Structural adjustment programs inhibits women's health, status, and educational and economic opportunities (Bradshaw, Noonan, Gash, & Sershen, 1993). In Kenya, the introduction of the cost-sharing strategy, a structural adjustment program, has had a negative impact on the education of girls and on the health of their mothers. The intensification of women's labor has led to an enormous degree of additional physical, mental, and emotional stress with adverse effects on their health and on the education of their children, particularly that of their daughters.

The structural programs are not implemented in a vacuum. The pressure to repay the debts by the international community has meant heavy sacrifices. As Mwalimu Julius Nyerere (former president of Tanzania) observed, children are starving so that countries can pay their debts. UNICEF notes that "hundreds of thousands of developing world's children have given their lives to pay their countries' debts, and many millions more are still paying the interest with their malnourished minds and bodies" (1989). Women, unfortunately, have to take up the challenge and try to create opportunities for their children in the midst of this sociological crisis. In the midst of these harsh conditions, women have reached out to traditional principles of organizing and are working as a collective in the form of self-help groups to afford their children educational opportunities. These women's groups are discussed in the next chapter.

9

"Help Me So That I May Help You"
∯ ∯ ∯ ∯
Women's Self-Help Movement

The women's discourse on education shows that their educational and economic opportunities are limited by cultural, social, and economic factors. It also shows women's agency in their effort to offer their children, and daughters in particular, educational opportunities. Mothers have been working very hard to provide their daughters with educational opportunities because they know the importance of education. The women pointed out that they left school against their wishes since they lacked intervention agents to support them in their struggle to obtain educational skills. Thus the women are doing whatever is possible to give their children educational opportunities.

Women realize that without education, their children, and daughters in particular, will not be able to be self-reliant and to break out of the poverty into which they were born. The women's efforts are not recognized, and they are not receiving support to intervene in their children's education in more effective and meaningful ways. The government does not seem to be aware of, or does not recognize, the increasing burden that women and parents are bearing to educate their children. The implementation of the structural adjustment programs are hurting the poor, and these happen to be women and their dependents. These programs have a negative impact on the health of the women and especially on the education of girls. Even though the women have "sacrificed" themselves to offer their children educational opportunities denied them, the demands on the women are overwhelming. Their efforts are hampered by cultural, economic, environmental, and political factors.

However, as Dei (1995) observed, "village women have been known to rely on long established traditions of community solidarity, based on traditional principles of group mutuality to help to relieve the economic pain of households" (p. 12). In Kenya,

> women's self-help groups have flourished as a means for women to cope creatively with the sweeping post-independence economic and social change and with the exigencies of a neocolonial political economy. . . . The practice of cooperation and the discourse of communality surviving from precolonial times animates the women's contemporary self-help groups. (Stamp, 1995, p. 73)

Women's self-help groups in the traditional setting became necessary as a collective geared at identifying a task and at putting their resources together to work on the task. "The concept of groups was based on mutual social responsibility, accountability and reciprocity" (Republic of Kenya: Women's Bureau/SIDA Project, 1992). In precapitalist Africa, women came together to promote their common economic, political, and social interests. Colonialism and urbanization, however, undermined many of these associations, leaving women in a much less powerful position than men (House-Midamba, 1996; Wipper 1995). Women's self-help groups in Ukambani are similar to the traditional "working parties" or *myethya* (Hill, 1991).

The majority of present-day women's groups are self-help groups. The original objectives and aims have changed to accommodate the rapid political and socioeconomic changes. Women's groups are seen as a force to improve the position of rural women in Kenya since they contribute substantially to raising standards of living and to bringing infrastructure to rural areas. In 1992, there were about 23,614 women's groups in Kenya (UNICEF/GOK, 1992).

The government mandates that women's self-help groups be registered with the Women's Bureau, Ministry of Social Services. The registration enhances the government's control over the political activities of these groups. Women's groups are not supposed to engage in politics particularly aligning themselves with opposition parties. One Kilome group that has association with the controversial leader of the Green Belt movement have had to conceal this association for political reasons. They maintain two separate records—one for government purposes and the other for their Green Belt movement.

Many groups have had to register themselves with the Women's Bureau to legalize their group meetings since the government has made it illegal to hold a gathering without a permit from the divisional president's office. Women's self-help groups that are registered with this bureau also stand a better chance of getting aid from International Development agencies channeled through the bureau. The Women's Bureau was set up in 1975 to coordinate government policies toward women through the "Women's Group Program." Feldman (1983) points out that the Women's Bureau serves to legitimate certain kinds of "special treatment" for women on the grounds that women have been disadvantaged in the past. These special programs are initiated, controlled, or coordinated by government agencies, while women's self-help groups' activities are initiated and controlled by the women themselves.

During my fieldwork, I worked with three women's self-help groups, namely Kithumba, Kyandue, and Salama women's self-help groups in Kilome division. These groups were set up by the women from these villages to address their own identified concerns. Kyandue women's self-help group is the oldest among the three groups. Kithumba and Salama groups were formed during the research process by the women who participated in this study.

Kyandue Women's Self-Help Group

Kyandue village has one major women's self-help group that is divided into sections A and B (Rachel & Meli, Interview, July 1994). The groups operate as a single group or as two entities, depending on the nature of the tasks. The group functions as a single group when they engage in such community work as building gabions. One section of this group is composed of women married to men belonging to the Ambua clan. This group was formed out of a tragedy, and its primary role is to formalize those marriages in the Ambua clan that had not been formalized and to ensure that future marriages carried out in this clan are formalized.

In the traditional setting, the process of "sealing" or of formalizing the marriage relationship was long. It began when a young man and his family were accepted as suitable suitors by the bride's family. Two goats (male and female) were sent to the in-laws-to be. Along with them went a leather strap (Muthiani, 1973, p. 26). Other gifts followed, but the most important ones were the two goats, which were sent by the young man's parents and relatives. In Kyandue, the women are taking charge of the situation and ensuring that the marriage relationships are sealed not only to prevent burial disputes but also to ensure that their children's lineage is not threatened. Rachel describes the circumstances that led to the formation of her group.

Ra: We try to formalize marriages as they should have been done traditionally by paying bridewealth [*kuasan'ya*[1]]. People have stopped paying bridewealth as they used to and this is bringing a lot of problems today.

MN: Why would you want to pay bridewealth for each other?

Ra: What made us to insist on formalizing marriages is because one woman married in our clan died and there was a big problem because her husband had not even taken the two goats to her parents. So, her people wanted to bury her and our man also wanted to bury her and here were the children caught in between. It was very sad and so anyway, our clan had to contribute money and items to take to the deceased woman's parents so that we could bury her. When we looked around, we realized that our deceased cowife was not the only one whose marriage had not been formalized. In fact, I was the first one to have my marriage formalized by this women's self-help group. I was married in 1977 and the two goats that are taken to the bride's parents were taken there in 1989. How many years are those? The group said that they were not going to stay with somebody's daughter without having gone to see her parents. It is also a sign of respect to the woman's parents. The members of the group bought six goats, maize, beans, and other items to take to my parents [*kumova mukwa*[2]]. The whole process is taken very seriously. (Interview, July 1994)

The payment of bridewealth has been interpreted by many scholars, particularly feminists, as a practice that causes women to be treated as a man's personal property and reinforces their subordination to men. I must admit that I was shocked to hear that Kyandue women were not only initiating the process but were also providing the resources required to complete the process. However, the women saw the process as one of honoring the parents of the bride and one that brought respect for the bride. This process also ensures that children born by the woman belong to the husband's clan. This gives the children the right to inherit their father's property. In the Kyandue incident, if the woman's parents had buried her, they would have the right to keep her children under customary law. This would have been a loss to the husband, his family, and the clan. Mbiti observes that bridewealth is a gift given as a token of gratitude on the part of the bridegroom's people to those of the bride, for their care over her and for allowing her to become his wife. The marriage gift is an important institution in African societies (Mbiti, 1990, p. 137).

The Kyandue women's group also engages in many other activities besides formalizing marriages. The group's activities are also geared toward increasing food security and providing support for women and for their children, as well as for increasing women's income. The group members plant bananas for each other. Women from Kyandue had learned from previous famines that you could die with money in your pocket; therefore these women decided to start planting bananas. The women came to this decision as a group as they met to discuss ways to combat future famines.

I am the chairman of the group. Since we got together we decided to plant bananas so that when it gets dry and there is a food shortage we can cook for our children these bananas. When the rains fail women experience a lot of difficulties trying to feed their children. You have to have money to buy food and sometimes you can have the money and then you find that there is no food in the shops. I am sure you can remember the previous famine which people branded I'm dying with money in my pocket [*nikw'a ngwete*]. Also, you know how bananas are in demand these days? So women can also sell these bananas when they get ready. (Interview, July 1994)

Rachel, who is an official of a Kyandue women's self-help group, points out that her group's motto is Help Me so that I May Help You, and this has worked very well. She has benefited from the bananas that this group helped her plant. At the time of this study, Kyandue women's groups had 3,000 Kenya shillings (U.S. $60) in their savings account. They felt that their group did not have a large savings account because members are poor and also because the group did not have a sponsor so that they could acquire funds to boost its projects from the Women's Bureau or from any aid organization. The women planned to use the money to buy maize during the harvesting season when it was inexpensive and then to resell it during the dry season when the demand and prices are higher. They were also making money by hiring out their services. They carried bricks for people, tilled the land, and fetched firewood.

The Kyandue self-help group has not attracted aid from the various government or from nongovernmental agencies as some groups have. As Urdvardy (1988) observes, the process of nominating a women's self-help group for a grant from the Women's Bureau is time-consuming and I would say, corrupt. Often, there are more groups nominated than there are funds available.

The Kyandue women's group uses its money to create possibilities and to offer options to its members. As Meli, the chairperson observed, helping each other is consistent with the goals of their group.

> Me: We use the money to support our members in different ways, for example, one woman who lost her husband and wanted to sell a piece of land, we gave her the 2,000 Kenya shillings [U.S. $35] she needed so that she wouldn't sell the land. We saw that land is hard to come by and therefore we discussed with her about better measures to undertake other than that one of selling land.
>
> Helping women is in line with our goals because when we started the group, the goal and purpose was to support each other so that our women do not have to sell valuable things like land when faced with emergencies such as death in the family. We also help to pay school fees. Recently we contributed 1,000 Kenya shillings [U.S. $18] for a member to take her child back to school after the child had been sent home to collect school fees balance. (Interview, July 1994)

The availability of bananas in Kyandue is a new phenomenon. The women told me that prior to the introduction of the self-help group, many women did not own a single banana plant. During my fieldwork, I learned from the women that the production of bananas in this village had already attracted banana buyers from other divisions and locations outside Kilome division. This has not only increased food security in this area but also has increased the women's income.

The women's group's ability to adapt and to respond to the changing social, economic, environmental, and political changes is a great asset. Unlike Kyandue women, many women's self-help groups focus primarily on such objectives as obtaining credit, generating income, and/or improving water supplies (UNICEF/GOK,

1992). The Kyandue women's group feels that they are capable of playing a central role in the education of their daughters by expanding the vision of their self-help group. Kyandue women felt that they should make girls' education every woman's business. One woman noted that if mothers united *(twithiwe na ngwatanio)*, they can ensure that none of their daughters failed to go to high school because of school fees. She noted that the child's education should not just be the individual family's responsibility *(mwana usu ndethinya nyinya na ithe eweka)* so that we can begin to educate our daughters.

Kithumba Women's Self-Help Group

The need to form Kithumba women's self-help groups came from the women's realization that they could achieve more if they worked as a group. The impetus also came from Kithumba women realizing what Kyandue women's self-help groups were doing and their future goals. Kithumba women identified poverty as the major "ailment" common to almost all women in this village. Women's groups were seen as necessary to improve women's economic and political status. This would enable the group to offer their children, and daughters in particular, educational opportunities. As Kathleen observed, women are very innovative and can collaborate to address girls' educational needs. One mother, Mbete, noted:

> What I think we need to do is start a women's self-help group so that we can begin to talk about the problems that we face as a group. So, if it is the education of our daughters, we as mothers should all feel responsible and plan on how to deal with the problem. We need to challenge each other and be each others' eyes. (Interview, July 1994)

The group plans to provide credit to its members, some of whom are petty traders who cannot be given credit by financial institutions because rural women do not have collateral. The women have started buying soap at wholesale prices and selling it at retail prices but 1 Kenya shilling cheaper than in the shops to attract customers. The profit is kept in the women's self-help group's savings account. There is no maize mill in the area and the women are aiming at purchasing one that would bring them more income, give them more options, and give them more resources to enable their children to acquire a meaningful education (Ndoti, Interview, August

1994). The group would like to plant green vegetables if they could get help to drill a borehole[3] that would have enough water to enable them to plant kale *(sukumawiki)*, French beans for export, and tomatoes and cabbages for the local market and for their own consumption. The aim is for the women in the group to support each other in order to become self-reliant. They want to be able to take control of their children's needs, since the government does not seem to be interested in supporting the women. Some women who have tried to pursue government bursaries for their children have been frustrated. They desire to be self-reliant rather than to depend on anyone else, including the government. Unfortunately, the women's income—generating opportunities are limited by the lack of capital. Mulee's desire to be self-reliant can be shared by most women in Kilome division.

> Mu: I don't really follow up on what the government really does. What I always pray for is to get money; money that I can work or sweat for. If I could get about 50,000 Kenya shillings [$1,000] as capital I could do a lot of things so that by the end of the month I could earn about 3,000 shillings [U.S. $60]. That would be like a salary equivalent to that I would have gotten if I had gone to school and become a primary schoolteacher? Knowing very well that what you are doing will get you about 3,000 Kenya shillings [U.S. $70]. I want to be able to plan for my children knowing that I am able to support them myself and not relying on handouts. (Interview, July 1994)

The women also express the need to use their group meetings to discuss issues that affect them. These include violence against women and women's health. We discussed AIDS/HIV, which the women felt was extremely important to discuss as it affects women, and most women do not have radios to listen to for current information. More importantly, the women, as members of a self-help group had become comfortable with each other so that they could ask questions and share information. They noted that there is a big gap between themselves, policymakers, and those who claim to speak on their behalf. They observed that elite women who claim to speak for rural women do not have a clue of how women's life is at the grassroots level. As Manduu noted "we have never seen any of them come to the village to talk with us here. They know where women can be found; we are in the villages!" (Interview, July 1994)

One issue with which the women are concerned about is the treatment they receive from doctors in hospitals. They noted that most doctors don't seem to respect them at all as women and mothers. Many women lamented that many doctors and even nurses do not treat women with dignity and tend to treat them as though they are "dirty." The women would like to carry new needles to hospitals to ensure their safety (Kithumba Women Group, August 1994). Collaboration between the women and increased income was seen as the only possibility of achieving these goals. The women are committed to succeed against insurmountable odds.

Salama Women's Self-Help Group

Prior to the inception of the research project, Salama did not have a women's group. As Beth, a resident pointed out, people in Salama, as in other urban settings, lead "atomistic" lives. Salama has no business or welfare associations. Vendors choose what to sell and where to set up their tables.

It is understandable why Salama town did not have a women's self-help group prior to my entry into the site. The individualistic life-style that women and men lead in Salama is characteristic of urban areas. Nevertheless, ten women from Salama, together with three men, noted the importance of a group in addressing issues confronting them. Among their pressing needs was girls' education. Poverty was seen as one factor that was steering girls away from school.

The Salama women indicated that it is important for people not to forget their traditional principles of collaboration. They noted that, traditionally, people worked together for the betterment of the community. There was an emphasis on collaboration as exemplified in sayings such as One Finger Cannot Kill a Louse. The women felt that the formation of women's self-help groups in Salama was long overdue.

When the group was formed, each member was asked to pay a membership fee of 140 Kenya shillings ($2.75) within a period of one week. The women decided to build a kiosk for selling boiled eggs and cold drinks in front of the market. The kiosk bore the name of the group—Salama Women Development Group. This small progress attracted many women to the group. Membership was dependent upon the consensus of all group members.

The Salama women's self-help group has major goals. The group intends to buy a maize mill that would bring them a better income if well managed. Salama has only one maize mill, and this forces women to wait in long queues for hours to have their maize milled. The women feel that a maize mill would improve their standard of living and enable them to offer their children better educational and economic opportunities.

Successes and Limitations

A large number of women's self-help groups disband within a short period of their creation. The Kyandue women's self-help group has been in operation for about two years and its achievements are concrete. For Kithumba and Salama women's groups, the momentum is high. Kithumba women had completed the handicrafts they were making during the first two months of the group's inception. The women made traditional Kenyan baskets, sisal ropes, and table clothes. The ropes were bought by members for carrying loads and for tethering livestock. A certain percentage of the sales was placed in the women's savings account.

The Salama women's self-help group was diversifying its business very rapidly. The group sought registration with the Women's Bureau, and they have already opened a savings account with Kenya Commercial Bank. The group has hired a woman to sell products in their kiosk and they have saved over 7,000 Kenya shillings ($150).

One major limitation faced by the women's groups is patronage by men. The patron-client relationship can be formed between the women's self-help groups and certain males, affecting the independence and success of the women's groups. Urdvardy (1988) notes incidents in Kilifi where men involved themselves with women's self-help groups because of the greater access that these groups have to development aid. Furthermore, the women not only constitute a necessary component but also a convenient labor force (p. 223).

Women's self-help groups' autonomy is limited by politicians who want to control them for their political ends, for instance, Kithumba and Salama women's groups were experiencing pressure from the local ruling party representative who vowed to alienate the groups' activities if they were found to be supporters of opposition parties. The representative claimed that these two groups were formed to solicit votes for an opposition candidate in the upcoming general elections.

Politicians' interference with women's self-help groups limits women's autonomy and also limits the people the group can call upon to support them in their projects or for a fund-raising drive.

Many women's groups do not want to be declared "controversial" or to have political affiliations with opposition groups. Such ties limit aid to these groups from the government or from international aid organizations who fear being accused of interfering in a country's internal affairs.

The activities of these women's self-help groups in Kilome division are limited by the capital they can raise through their income-generating activities and through their monthly contributions. As the women observed, they have not been able to attract any grants from the government or from aid organizations. They need funds to purchase a mill to increase their income to meet the educational needs of their children. They also would like support to drill a borehole in order to get water for irrigation. All these activities need credit, to which the women have no access. The women are not aware of how they can access aid money that has been made available to other women's self-help groups to fund similar projects. In addition, they do not have information on accessing credit from financial institutions. Even with such information, these women cannot get loans from financial institutions; loans require collateral, which they do not have.

The women's self-help groups' potential for addressing issues of concern to themselves and their children is impeded by internal and external factors. The paradox is that these groups are supposed to be apolitical and yet have political affiliations with the ruling party! However, these groups need autonomy in their efforts to meet the educational needs of their children. Any support given to them by government or by nongovernmental organizations should be "unattached." The support should not be for "development" projects as conceptualized by the government or by development organizations. As Dei (1995) argues, "development should speak to the social, economic, political, spiritual and cosmological aspects of local peoples' lives, as well as their specific needs and aspirations. It should reflect the lived realities, goals and aspirations of grassroots people" [women] (p. 16).

Exclusiveness of Women's Self-Help Groups

As a participant in the women's group, I learned that, although membership is open to all women, the conditions of membership exclude a large number of women, for example, some women are not able to keep up with the weekly, biweekly, or monthly contributions that are expected of members. Rose has limited her participation in women's self-help groups because of this factor. In fact, she dropped out of a Kithumba women's group, as she could not afford to make the weekly contributions. Rose noted the following:

R. I belong to one group called Maka Weka [worry alone]. I try not to join many groups because it is expensive to do so and my income is almost nothing. The group I participate in, we fill the canyon with stones and we are given food once in awhile. The group is associated with the Catholic Church. We also have had to pay 80 Kenya shillings [$1.60] to pay a watchman to look after the maize.

MN: How do you get money?

Ro: I only get money if I have a banana bunch that I ripen and sell it. This happens once in a very long time. (Interview, August 1994)

Kasika from Kyandue had a similar reason for not joining Kyandue women's self-help groups. She pointed out that "one needs land and money to participate in these groups. I have very little land and no space to plant bananas and so I couldn't join this group although it is good for me to do so but I cannot afford it" (Interview, July 1994). The government's demand for women's self-help groups to be registered with the Women's Bureau increases the pressure for these groups to raise money. To register, each group must pay 170 Kenya shillings ($3.50) for a certificate. When there is an harambee (a fund-raising drive), women's groups have to contribute a certain amount. When I was in Kenya, each women's group in Kilome division was expected to raise 1,500 Kenya shillings ($30) toward an harambee that was to be chaired by the minister of foreign affairs. All this money had to come from the women. As Ngina observed, "a woman must find a way of making her own money because if she always has to beg from her husband to make these contributions, he will not tolerate that begging and soon he'll ask her to leave the groups" (Interview, July 1, 1994).

The membership fee for the Salama women's self-help group also is too high for many women to afford. A membership fee of 175 Kenya shillings ($2.50) is inhibitive for a lot of women. However, Salama women insisted that this figure was the basic amount they needed to start a small business. Several women noted that these rates were too high for them because they did not have a source of income and/or have access to land where they could plant vegetables for income. Present-day women's self-help groups exclude the poorest women who need the group's help the most (JASPA, 1981). The women's desire not to rely on government handouts for their projects unfortunately eliminates those poor women who cannot afford to raise the membership fees.

Conclusion

In this chapter, I highlighted the potential and limitations for women's agency as a collective in the form of women's self-help groups. These groups are ubiquitous throughout rural Kenya and have been formed on traditional principles of mutual interdependence. As Stamp (1995) observes, these groups flourish as a means for women to cope creatively with sweeping postindependence economic and social change and with the exigencies of neocolonial political economy.

The groups have the potential to address issues concerning women's education, since the groups are based on the practice of cooperation and communality. As the women observed, girls in Kilome division continue to experience gender-related difficulties in accessing educational opportunities. The women know the importance of education and aspire to give their daughters educational skills to enable them to participate in the modern economy. They realize that their efforts to educate their children are limited by a lack of resources. On the other hand, they see their potential as a group in supporting each other in their efforts to meet their children's needs. They recognize the importance of identifying issues that concern them and plan ways to achieve solutions. The women's self-help groups that I worked with have made great progress toward achieving their goals. However, these groups' activities are limited by lack of credit. The women's income-generating activities could be improved if they had capital. However, women cannot get loans from any financial institutions because they do not have collateral. The women see their unity as a collateral that they can utilize to solicit financial support in the form of loans in a similar fashion as the Grameen Bank of Bangladesh. This bank gives loans to landless, assetless women who form a group that acts as a collateral. The group ensures that a member who takes out a loan from the bank repays it (YUNUS, 1991).

Present-day women's self-help groups, however, tend to eliminate the poor women who do not have access to land and money to make the weekly contributions. These groups are also affected by political interference that limits their activities and affiliations. However, as Ahlberg-Maina (1991) observes, women's self-help groups in rural Kenya are still an important resource for change. Women have continued to exploit the power of collective action in order to counteract negative forces within the system, even after colonial forces had disrupted their culture and collective organization. Ahlberg-Maina stresses that:

> The continued collective participation of women has not just offered a link between the past and the present, it constitutes a process of consciously selecting positive cultural traits and adapting them to meet new challenges. It is perhaps only through such dynamic participation that issues which evoke resistance can become an integral part of the collective activity and social order. (P. 187)

Stamp (1986) argues that women's self-help groups are not simply cooperative development projects, or strategies for coping with change; rather, they are vital organizations for resistance to exploitation. Women have become agents of resistance and change in the maelstrom of contemporary Kenyan affairs, for instance, some women in this study noted that they have shifted their labor to subsistence agriculture because they have more control over the food products than cash crop productions. Despite the shortcomings of the self-help groups, it is evident that the women's agency resides in their communal endeavors and is constantly reinvented in the context of political and social changes (Stamp, 1995).

10

Women's Educational Experiences

✂ ✂ ✂ ✂

Private and Public Discourses on
Education in Kenya and Implications for Policy

In this chapter I examine the public discourse on education of
women and men articulated in Kenyan policy documents in light
of the women's private discourse on education constructed from
the interviews with the rural women of Kilome division. I juxta-
pose the women's perception of themselves and the purpose of their
education with the envisioning of women held by predominantly
male policy makers. The women's discourse shows a strong belief
in the relationship between education and economic development.
They see higher education as the key to self-reliance, and they
struggle to provide their children with this level of education. The
women "sacrifice" themselves to afford their children educational
opportunities that otherwise would not be available to them. They
see a lack of access to educational opportunities as the greatest
impediment to self-reliance. While the women identify the gender-
related factors that limit their participation in education and in the
economy, they do not envision systematic ways of challenging the
institutionalized structures that continue their subordination.

Public and Private Discourses on Education

The public discourse regarding the purpose of the education of
women and men in Kenya is set out by predominantly male poli-

ticians and policy makers, and is influenced by international development agencies such as the World Bank. In the formulation of educational policies, gender issues are either framed in ways that confine women's agency to the private sphere and fail to challenge the gender and power factors that impede women's agency in the public sphere alongside men. Consequently, the factors that limit women's participation in education and in the public sphere remain invisible. The implementation of the ensuing seemingly gender-neutral policies has negative implications for women's education and reinforces existing gender inequities in Kenya.

An examination of the public discourse on education articulated in policy documents produced in Kenya in the past three decades since independence (1964–1993) shows that gender has been framed in ways that limit women's agency in the Kenyan society. The policy framings that have limited women's access to education include: gender neutrality, perception of women as reproducers and men as producers, educational policies produced by predominantly male policy makers, and nationalist policies of equal education and economic opportunities that failed to address gender and class issues.

While some policy documents assumed a gender-neutral perspective in the formulation of educational policies, others limited women's agency to the private sphere where they are "biologically responsible for bearing and rearing of children." Other policy documents recommended policies that would exclude an overwhelmingly majority of women. As Staudt and Parpart (1989) posit, women's seemingly personal, everyday experiences are structured by policies most of which are outwardly "gender-neutral" but are in fact experienced differently by men and women. Therefore, women, who have been systematically relegated to a private noneconomic sphere created in the colonial era, and inherited, maintained, and developed in the postcolonial era, have had different experiences of these policies than do men. This women's agency has continued to be marginalized into the private sphere. The Kenyan state, and the economy, education, and political systems it inherited and developed, are overwhelmingly controlled by men, and this control has translated into laws, policies, and spending patterns that not, coincidentally, benefit men. Male dominance in the public and private sphere impedes women's attempts to create possibilities for their children in Kenya today.

Staudt (1987) points out that nationalist movements, by their very nature, focus on the struggle for independence, rather than on gender or class interests. The goals of the nationalist movement in

Kenya were no different. At independence, the demands of the Africans for equal educational and employment opportunities were paramount. These demands were reflected in the educational policy recommendations of the first Kenya Education Commission, commonly known as the "Ominde Report of 1964." The emphasis in the Ominde Report was equity for the "African race" that had been discriminated against in accessing opportunities in the colonial period. Policies were recommended by predominantly male policy makers and implemented to ensure that the image reflected in public institutions and in the formal employment sector was African. This was made possible through the implementation of the Africanization policy designed to Africanize formal institutions in Kenya. No equivalent gender equity policies were provided to address women's unequal access to educational and economic opportunities initiated by the colonial administration that provided education along both race and gender lines.

At independence, few women got the opportunity to train for the high-level skills required for economic growth and Africanization of the formal employment sector. The policy makers, predominantly men, certainly did not see women as major players in the public space of economic activity. By this time, women's role in the public space was insignificant, since colonial policies had succeeded in making the public sphere the world of men by confining women to the private sphere where they increasingly became dependent on men. The image or perception of men as "producers" and of women as "reproducers" and dependents of men certainly influenced the policy makers who did not offer women opportunities to acquire the high-level skills needed to participate in the modern sector. Consequently, policymakers formulated policies that reinforced the legacy of women's low participation in the public sphere that has been carried over to the present day where women form only 22% of the formal employment sector. The emphasis at independence was, therefore, to address the race issue, and educational policies were formulated to "revolutionarize" the public sphere from a predominantly white male image to a predominantly African male image. The assumed gender-neutral policies promoted and reinforced gender inequities in postcolonial Kenya.

Since independence, much of the public discourse on education has emphasized provision of only basic education to women. Educational reports have emphasized the role of basic education for improving women's productivity in the informal sector. The public policy discourse also has emphasized basic education for enhancing women's delivery of gender-specific services as mothers, wives, and child bearers and rearers. The public discourse has continued to portray women as biologically responsible for bearing and rearing of children and therefore solely responsible for the reproductive labor. Policy makers have recommended that women be given basic education to help slow the population growth in Kenya. This image of women as "biologically" responsible for childbearing and rearing has made them targets of population control programs and has relieved men of responsibility over their role in procreation and has placed the entire burden and labor on the shoulders of women whose work loads have tremendously increased. It is upon this logic that school girls who conceive while at school are sent away without hope of ever reentering the school system.

Rural women emphasized the need for their daughters to acquire higher educational skills that can afford them economic independence and self-reliance. The women note that marriage is no longer a solution and that a woman can no longer depend on a man to meet the needs of her family. The rural women want their daughters to be able to lead less strenuous lives than they themselves. They know that basic education has restricted their participation to the private sphere where they face enormous constraints in their efforts to provide the basic needs for their children.

The women of Kilome emphasized the need for their daughters to get an education that can lead to paid employment. They see higher education as capable of giving their daughters the opportunity to enjoy what Mann (1995) refers to as the social enfranchisement of women. With social enfranchisement, the scope of the women's agency changes as they enter the public sphere as economic and political agents alongside men. These women want their daughters to be able to make individuated rational choices about their social, economic, and political destiny, as do men. Like the Chagga women of northern Tanzania (Stambach, 1998), Kilome women want their daughters to be in a position to choose whether to get married or to remain single. The women are opposed to their conditions of existence, which are characterized by dependence, subservience, and insignificant economic roles. They want their daughters to participate in the world of those who own and control property and who are active participants in the modern state (Staudt, 1987). The women are aware of how their agency to provide for their children has been limited by the sexual division of labor outside and within procreation and between procreation and production (Jaggar, 1983). These women, however, do not propose radical measures to address the structures that continue their subordination.

The women's discourse on the role of education in economic development supports the policy discourse on the role of education in development. However, their belief that education leads to paid employment in the modern sector is not supported by most policy documents that emphasize education for rural development or for vocationalization of education for self-employment. Their strong belief in the importance of education is matched by the activities that women are engaged in as mothers to provide their children with educational opportunities. They are engaged in a multiplicity of activities to earn income to meet the ever-increasing costs of education instituted by the government through the cost-sharing policies.

Kilome women identify the factors that limited their participation in education as well as those that continue to limit girls' educational opportunities in Kilome. They note that poverty is the major factor that is denying their children, and daughters in particular, educational opportunities and thus limiting their chances of participating in the formal employment sector. The women do not question the structural factors that have enabled the creation of the impoverished conditions they live in. Rather, they are determined to "sacrifice" themselves to do their best to afford their daughters educational and economic opportunities denied them by social, cultural, economic, and political factors. They identify high school fees, gendered assumptions about girls' sexuality—potential motherhood, and, pregnancy rates among high primary and secondary-level girls as some of the factors that limit Kilome girls' educational opportunities. While the women identify these impediments, they do not envision radical ways of challenging the structures that maintain them. However, they see educational opportunities as capable of facilitating a silent revolution. The women's actions are not simply ones of collusion or adaptation to exploitative and oppressive situations; rather, they also act in resistance to the power relations that continue their subordination.

The increasing school fees being charged in secondary schools are a major barrier to girls' education. As one participant pointed out, at present the education of girls is worse off than it was a decade ago. Fewer girls are able to complete the secondary level of education. Mothers know that a primary level education does not offer the resources that enables one to be self-reliant. This is true of the experience of a good number of the women who participated in the study on which this book is based. They received seven years of primary education but have not found any meaningful income-generating opportunities. These women have been relegated to the private sector where they are solely responsible for subsistence production.

Policy makers did not highlight the barriers that women encounter in accessing educational opportunities; rather, the policy makers recommended an increase of parents' responsibility over the education of their children through the cost-sharing strategy. The implementation of this policy has tremendously increased the demand for women's material and physical labor and has had a negative impact on girls' education. Kilome women noted that, more than ever before, more parents are having to make choices about whose education is worth investing in. In almost all the cases, the choice has been to invest in the education of boys because girls are still considered "transient."

These rural women have "sacrificed" themselves to offer their daughters educational opportunities to increase their employability. They see education as a tool that their daughters could use to make choices: whether or not to get married, own property, and support their mothers and families. These women's work, however, has increased tremendously as they have picked up new roles and challenges in a gendered economy.

The women's sources of income include employment as casual laborers, sale of farm produce, and involvement in petty business; in addition, they participate in women's self-help groups. In addition, the women's labor is required for food production, and rearing and for caring for children, the sick, and the aged. The policy discourse does not highlight how women's labor subsidizes men and capital, both of which enable men's participation in a cash economy, particularly in the formal employment sector. It does not indicate that the women's unpaid labor is the backbone of economic development. Rural women provide the physical and material labor to build schools and to provide the resources their children require to acquire education for participation in the economy. However, even one of the most gender-sensitive reports, the Ndegwa Report (1991), offers little opportunity for women's unpaid labor in the private sphere to be equally matched with services by the state to improve women's living conditions. The Ndegwa Report claimed that "women's contribution to development has been widely acknowledged in official policy statements and development literature" (p. 229). The contribution to economic development deserves more than acknowledgment. The mere disclosure of women's contribution to development neither addresses the subordination and domination that women experience, nor the impoverished living conditions of most of the rural women. Meaningful acknowledgment should be matched with relevant policies to minimize women's exploitation and to ease their daily struggle in their attempts to create possibilities for their children.

The Ndegwa Report further claims that the government has directed significant efforts at measures for promoting women's development and for redressing the disadvantages suffered by women during the colonial period especially due to the neglect of their education. Although participation of girls in the primary level has reached parity to that of boys, statistics show that the dropout rate of girls in this level is about 60%. Girls are still faced with a multitude of barriers in their attempt to access educational opportunities. The government's implementation of the cost-sharing strategy has worsened the situation by increasing parents' contributions to their children's education. One participant observed that the implementation of the cost-sharing strategy has certainly reduced the number of girls, particularly those from poor families in the rural areas, in achieving meaningful educational opportunities. The women's self-sacrificial income-generating activities are limited. Most of them cannot provide their daughters with meaningful educational opportunities.

The Ndegwa Report called on Kenya to implement the Convention of all Forms of Discrimination Against Women to which it is a signatory. It also called for an increase in the number of opportunities for women in key positions in private and public sectors of the formal employment sectors.[1] Who benefits from such policies if they are implemented? Such policies benefit a small number of women and exclude the overwhelming majority of rural women and ordinary women-workers.

Staudt (1987) argues that while women share commonalities from their reproductive capacities, obvious differences exist among women based on their class position and resulting differences in opportunities and life-styles. Staudt argues that women have not been universally disadvantaged. She points out that

Given the near universal advantages of those with more education, money, land and in politics, women with those resources are politically advantaged and can acquire skills appropriate in given regimes along with a sense of "winnable" political goals. . . . Their winnability narrows the political agenda to demands compatible with the conception of women that the regime can accommodate. Very rarely do women activists in conventional politics articulate genuinely redistributive issues. . . . Should the wealthier women take

162   $\mathscr{S}$ *Women's Agency and Educational Policy*

up this redistributive issue in Kenya's zero-sum politics, more for other women would mean less for themselves. Their economic stakes lie more in their households than in solidarity with other women. (P. 203)

The Ndegwa Report was produced with the input of two high-ranking women academics. One had been the chairperson of the Maendeleo Ya Wanawake Organization (Progress for Women movement). It is not possible to know whether these women attempted to put through policies that would make rural women's lives less of a sacrifice but were overruled by a predominantly male commission. What is clear is that the policy recommendation outcomes did little to lessen the burdens that rural women endure in their attempt to meet the basic needs of their families. The commissioners did not recommend redistributive policies that would give women in the rural communities access to resources such as land, credit, and water to ensure food security and income from sale of cash crops and excess farm produce. More importantly, the report failed to address the structures that have made such conditions possible. In addition, the report did not challenge the gender-biased ownership policies and laws stipulated in the Sessional Paper # 10 of 1965 that denied women ownership and control of property, particularly land. The right to own land and therefore acquire credit was systematically passed onto men who were assumed to be heads of households. The issuance of land title deeds to these men gave them absolute control over the land, its products, and its disposal, even against the will of the wife.

In addition, the Ndegwa Report, which these two high-ranking female academics helped produce, proposed support for women in home-based activities such as tailoring and food processing rather than policies to improve small-scale farming that would improve the lives of the 80% of the women living in the rural areas. Besides such policies reinforcing the public-private distinctions, they also benefit the local elite since the ensuing sewing programs are likely to be both irrelevant and time-consuming for the majority of women who are engaged in a multiplicity of activities as food producers, petty traders, and care givers (Staudt, 1987).

Throughout the thirty years, most policy makers have formulated policies without considering their impact on women, for instance, unemployment became a social, economic, and political concern when an overwhelmingly number of men began to crowd the urban areas in search of unavailable employment. The Mackay, Wanjigi, and Kamunge Reports (1981–1983, and 1988) recommended and emphasized a rural-development focus to curb the rural-urban migration. Also recommended was a continual vocationalization of school subjects in order for school graduates to become self-employed. None of these reports examined (or recommended examination of) the impact of these policies on women if men remained in the rural areas particularly in connection with access to resources such as land. From the study it became clear that women utilize the limited land accessible to them to plant food crops and other crops for sale. Women do not benefit from growing cash crops, although their labor produces these cash crops—an exploitation that some women have resisted in subtle ways as in relegating their energies in planting food crops. It is clear that with more men having to depend on land for income, women's access to land will be adversely limited. This will also affect food security, as men are likely to engage in cash crop production. This would ultimately impact female education, as men would demand women's labor for cash crop production. They would also have direct access to the incomes and would not likely spend it on their families' welfare, particularly on their daughters' education.

Policy makers saw vocationalization of school subjects for self-employment as a panacea for the looming high unemployment rates. The reports recommended the introduction of courses such as masonry, carpentry, and tailoring. In order for a school graduate to become self-employed he or she will have to purchase the equipment. In addition to the credit limitations, the courses provided are likely to attract boys, since they are traditionally male fields.

Despite the policy recommendations on self-employment and provision of vocational subjects, Kilome women seem to believe strongly that economic independence can only become possible through paid employment, particularly in the formal employment sector. The women are not aware of the high unemployment rates and the discrimination that their daughters might face in the labor market. What is important to them right now is to provide their daughters with educational opportunities that give them a chance to "knock on the doors" of the modern employment sector. The women's agency is not just centered around motherhood, but they participate in economic roles that go a long way to make their children and spouses'/partners' economic activities in the public possible.

However the women's agency is limited by policies that do increase their burdens, such as the implementation of the cost-sharing strategy as a measure of structural adjustment programs. With this policy, the government has reduced spending on education and health services. The amount of fees that children have to pay at the secondary level is astronomical (25,000 Kenya shillings, or $500 per term). In addition to school fees, parents are expected to buy stationery, uniforms, and pay for other fees that might be deemed necessary. Mothers have stepped in as agricultural subsistence producers, petty traders, and workers to meet their children's educational needs. The women's economic activities are limited by the sexual division of labor assigning to them the responsibility of the bearing and caring of children, the sick, and the aged. In addition, women have limited access to resources. The intensification of their work load has threatened their health and their ability to provide for their children. Structural adjustment policies have a negative impact on the education of girls, and the demand to invest heavily in the education of girls has made more parents invoke gendered cultural beliefs to make choices on who is to be educated. Girls' educational opportunities are limited by the preference for boys in the provision of educational opportunities based on the gendered cultural assumptions of inherent motherhood and high pregnancy rates among senior primary and secondary-level girls. These are barriers that the policymakers do not address adequately.

Implications for Policy

In her examination of trends in women's education at the secondary and university levels in six sub-Saharan African (SSA) countries, Beoku-Betts (1998) concludes that there are serious gender-differentiated problems that must be addressed in policy and program planning in the educational sector. Educational and development policies play a critical role in fostering or perpetuating gender inequities in educational opportunities. Beoku-Betts notes that even though these policies may not be consciously framed to produce patterns of inequality, some of the indirect consequences resulting from these policies constrain women's ability to access and perform equitably within the system (p. 175).

This analysis of public policy discourse and the private discourse of the women in Kenya in relation to education shows that policy makers continue to formulate policies that limit women's agency to the private sphere of a gendered society. The policy makers seem to uphold the image of a society with distinctive public and private spheres divided along gender lines. This perception limits women's educational opportunities as they confine women to the private sphere, oblivious of the activities that women are undertaking to provide their children with educational opportunities.

The women's perception of themselves and of their daughters is different from that held by the policy makers. The women do not see their daughters' agency defined around motherhood only but rather as economic and political agents in the public sphere alongside men. The women identify lack of resources and gender-related barriers that limit girls' education. They also identify the patriarchal ideology that limit their agency as intervention agents. These are factors that the policy makers did not address. There is a need for the following changes to be effected to address some of the factors that limit girls' education. The changes include:

a. making gender and class equity issues pivotal in the policy-making process,

b. providing material and psychological support for girls' education starting at the village level,

c. granting opportunity for reentry of adolescent mothers into the school system and holding fathers of these children responsible for them,

d. reintroducing sex education in schools and communities, and

e. supporting women as intervention agents for their daughters' education as individuals and as groups.

The examination of the policy documents has shown that policymakers marginalize gender issues in the formulation of policies. This observation has also been made by Kibwana (1992), a law professor at the University of Nairobi who points out that official documents hardly concede to the issue of gender equity or sensitivity to women's issues. He notes that even in one of the most recent development plans (1989–1993), "women's role in Kenya society is fleetingly recognized" (p. 9). Planning and the development of policies and programs in Kenya have taken on the male perspective, since men have dominated the public sphere of policymaking and implementation. The policy makers see the world from the perspective of men rather than from the perspective of both men and women. This perception has reinforced gender inequities. Policies that have been formulated and implemented do not address the peculiar circumstances of both men and women. Instead, they have in most cases ended up favoring men (Kibwana, 1992).

There is need for policymakers to address gender equity issues in the formulation of educational policies in a gendered society. In addition, women need equal representation in the commissions and in working parties charged with policy formulation. Nzomo (1989) argues that it is only if women are well represented in policy-making bodies that they can influence policy changes necessary for their empowerment. It is not enough to have women representatives in commissions or in parliament. As Staudt and Glickman (1989) observe, privileged women who have represented women in these commissions and legislature have not advocated for policies that favor the rural and urban poor.

Resistance to gender and women's issues is so pervasive in the society that even politicians will make overtly sexists remarks and threats and expect no criticism from other politicians or from the head of their political party.[2] Hostility is vented out to women who challenge the state for formulating gender-insensitive policies. Often, these women are discredited by politicians and have been accused of being misled by Western feminist ideology. Stamp (1991) posits that:

The language of Western feminism is easily dismissed as yet another imperialist tool in the oppression of Third World people and a cause espoused by alienated and selfish elite African women. In this discourse, anti-imperialist ideology is articulated with right-wing and sexist political positions in a way that mystifies and discredits feminism and that stymies direct action in the name of women's rights. (P. 827)

The women's agency continues to be perceived as emanating from their roles as mothers, not as economic and political agents as men in the public sphere. Mathai (1991) observes that in Kenya "the sky is not the limit" for women; rather, gender, marriage, and culture are women's limits (quoted in Gruduah, 1991). The education system that is supposed to help inculcate attitudes on the equality and rights of all persons in Kenyan youth is not doing so, for instance, women who comprise 80% of the small-scale farmers are not represented as such in agriculture textbooks used in schools. Most girls are not choosing science and mathematics in high school (Eshiwani, 1990). Consequently, girls cannot pursue high-status careers in science and technology. Orientation of the education of girls/women is for low-status jobs or for the provision of unpaid labor, which only reinforces the subordination of women. The underrepresentation of girls and women in science and mathematics courses and science related careers is prevalent in many SSA countries (Beoku-Betts, 1998; Ndunda and Munby, 1991). In most of these countries, curricula are still structured to reinforce societal perceptions of women's role in family life (Beoku-Betts, 1998). Within the official circles, and in society at large, the level of gender sensitivity is exceedingly low. There is resistance, mostly by men, to the genderization of issues because it challenges their expectations and male hegemony. It challenges patriarchy in which men assume superiority over women (Kibwana, 1992; Nzomo, 1997). Women, as the majority of voters, must seek to elect women, who are sensitive to gender issues, to parliament in large numbers because it is in the parliament where the laws that influence women's lives are passed (Nzomo, 1989, 1997). Making gender a category of policy analysis means challenging deeply engrained gendered assumptions that reinforce gender inequities not only in education but also in the general society.

In addition to employing gender as a category of analysis, class and regional development issues must also be taken into consideration. As Mohanty (1991) points out, women are not a monolith. The impact of policies on middle-class urban women who are advantaged by education, money, and political power cannot be the same as those of the poor rural women who have no access to land, shelter, and money. Staudt (1987) argues that women with these advantages do acquire favors in given regimes. Colonial and postcolonial development policies along regional lines have created discrepancies in accessing educational and economic opportunities.

Regional development and climatic factors also influence the opportunities that are made available to women in Kenya. Urban areas and provinces such as the central province have the most developed infrastructures in Kenya. This legacy was inherited from the colonial government and was reinforced by the postcolonial government of Kenya. The central province is also the most arable region in Kenya. Therefore, ethnicity and region shape women's daily experiences differently, for instance, the International Labor Organization studies on employment opportunities for rural women gave the impression that most of these women can find work in plantations or in large-scale farms. This might be a reality for a few women who live in the 17% arable region of Kenya. Therefore, the impact of policies in relation to gender, class, and region must be examined, even though in the Sessional Paper # 10 (1965), Kenyan politicians and policymakers denied the existence of classism in the society. Addressing gender, class, and regional issues in policymaking is a great challenge to the status quo.

Support for Girls' Education Starting at the Village Level

The high school fees charged at the secondary levels of education are a great barrier to girls' educational opportunities. Some girls who have been admitted to government-maintained schools, which are well established and have facilities, equipment, qualified teachers, and extracurricula educational opportunities, have had to go to inferior quality harambee day schools that are relatively cheaper. Most harambee schools do not have qualified teachers and do not teach pure science subjects. Students' performance in the university entry examinations are poor in harambee schools. Therefore, it is important to ensure that girls who are admitted to government secondary schools make it into these schools. This can be facilitated through the establishment of a special fund. Information on how to access these funds should be made available to parents at the village level. At present, there is supposed to be a fund that helps needy children. During my fieldwork, I found that most rural women do not know of its existence, and those who know about it and have applied for funds were frustrated and intimidated by the lengthy time- and money-consuming and corrupt process, so they eventually gave up.

In addition, if a girl does not report to the secondary school after she has been admitted, it would be important for the head teacher to be aware of the circumstances surrounding this case. Often, girls will not show up at school because of lack of school fees, uniforms, even bus fare or early marriage. Head teachers are swift to give away vacancies that become available in this manner. It is important that the head teacher contact the parents/guardians through the divisional education office before the girl's place is given to somebody else. It could be that this girl's father has refused to invest in her education because he wants to wed her off or to send her to work as a house girl. There should be options available to ensure that such a girl goes to school.

Reentry of Adolescent Mothers into the School System

The number of adolescent mothers is on the increase (UNICEF/ GOK, 1992). Kilome women pointed out that many girls are leaving school because of pregnancy; this marks the end of their formal schooling. Schools do not readmit a girl who leaves school due to pregnancy because she is considered a bad role model. In addition to this reason for leaving school, pregnancy is a big disappointment to her parents, and most fathers, who pay school fees most of the time and allocate resources in the household, consider it "risky" to reinvest in the education of such a girl. Therefore, it becomes almost impossible for this girl to reenter the formal education system. Few SSA countries retain pregnant girls in school (Beoku-Betts, 1998). Dropping out of school limits the girl's educational and economic opportunities and she often ends up in a subordinated role in a marriage relationship. It is important that such girls are given a chance to continue with formal schooling without being discriminated against. It is also important that girls are given the space to talk about the circumstances that led to the pregnancies. Most of the time, there is an adult male involved, often a teacher, who admonishes the girl to remain silent. These men who abuse their power are often never brought to justice. Girls need to be provided with the channels and necessary skills to deal with such men. They need to be able to report sexual harassment and abuse without fear of being accused of provoking it. There is a need to deal with the double standard of victimizing girls who get pregnant while letting the men responsible for the pregnancies continue with their education or careers undisturbed. Tough laws need to be implemented for those adults who are responsible. At the moment, it is the responsibility of a rape victim to prove that she did not provoke it. This treatment has only served to silence the majority of rape victims. The stigma and psychological stress associated with teenage pregnancy has caused many teenage deaths as they attempt to procure illegal abortions. Addressing the issue of teenage pregnancy and the treatment of teenage mothers mandates that the patriarchy and its control of women's sexuality is challenged. Hartmann (1993) argues that patriarchy, a set of interrelations among men that allow men to dominate women, has a material base. The material base is men's control over women's labor power, and "that control is maintained by excluding women from access to necessary economically productive resources and by restricting women's sexuality" (p. 196).

Introducing Sex Education in Schools and Communities

The introduction of Western formal education and Christianity replaced traditional education in which grandmothers played crucial roles as sex educators. Since grandmothers lost their role and credibility as knowledgeable sex educators, they have not been replaced. Recent attempts to introduce sex education in schools have been impeded by religious groups and by parents who feel that sex education will make their daughters promiscuous. There is a need for a consensus on how this issue should be approached because teenage girls are getting pregnant and leaving school, and even worse they are dying. Most cases go unreported. Students, both boys and girls, need to be aware of their sexuality and of the responsibilities that go with it. There is need for girls to be made aware that they should not tolerate sexual harassment or abuse. I recommend that there be an adult who girls can trust to discuss sex-related matters without being made to feel "immoral." In the past, grandmothers represented that individual whom girls could trust. Schools can use individuals from the community, ranging from contemporary sex educators to traditional sex educators—grandmothers.

Support for Women as Intervention Agents for Their Daughters' Education

Mothers are involved in a multiplicity of activities in an effort to improve their families' living conditions and to provide their children with educational opportunities. The women's endeavors are impeded by the rising costs of living and by the implementation of structural adjustment policies that have meant less government funding for education and health services. Their efforts are also limited by the traditional sexual division of labor and limited access to resources. The activities that the women are engaged in are labor-intensive and bring them minimum profits that can barely meet their families' basic needs, not to mention educational needs. The rotating credit that the women's self-help groups operate provides its members with only temporary help because it is so infrequent. By the time the credit arrives, the woman has already accumulated huge debts and expenses, such as school and doctors' fees, which cannot be offset with a one-time credit.

The Kenya government, international donor countries, and development agencies have come to look upon women's self-help groups as the most viable organizational base for implementing women's projects ranging from social welfare to those dealing with income generation. Consequently, a lot of money has been made available to the government to channel to the women's projects. Unfortunately, this money does not seem to reach most women because of the politics of aid at the national and local levels. Nzomo (1989) argues that economic programs being promoted under the umbrella of women's groups have not enabled women to attain economic empowerment. In addition, the women's groups exclude over 60% of eligible women in Kenya. There are, however, various benefits that women enjoy from participating in women's groups, for example, they benefit from the social interaction group membership gives, since they get a chance to break away from their individual isolation and confinement in their respective homes and family-related activities. It is, however, important that these self-help groups be made more inclusive and independent from local and national government control. A few groups in semiarid areas have received credit and organizational skills from organizations such as the African Medical Research Foundation (AMREF) that have increased the groups' income tremendously.

The focus should be on individual women and to find out how they may be supported to support themselves. Lack of credit is a major barrier to their individual businesses. Women need to have access to credit. One method that has been adopted by a nongovernmental organization working in Kibwezi (defined as an opposition zone during the research period) is to provide credit to a self-help group for individual women. The group is the collateral, and the woman owes it to the entire group to repay back the loan. This method is the underlying principle behind the successful Grameen Bank in Bangladesh, which is run and owned by poor rural women. This bank was started by the economist Mohammed Yunus (Yunus, 1991).

Conclusion

In this chapter, I explored women's experiences of education from which I construed what I call "women's private discourse of education." I contrasted the women's discourse with the public discourse of education articulated in policy documents. Beyond the rural women's experiences of education, I examined the women's agency in their multiple subjectivity as mothers, sisters, daughters, workers, educators, and traders to understand how they perceive themselves and explain their actions. The women's self-perception counters the facile but popular imagery that reduces the African woman to an anguished, helpless mother holding a famished child (Stamp, 1995).

Rural women are not pawns. They are social actors and are responding to the social, economic, and political changes and are creating educational and economic possibilities for their children. Analysis of policy documents shows that women's agency is limited by policies.

While the women emphasize the acquisition of higher education for self-reliance, policymakers emphasize basic education to control reproduction and hopefully to provide self-employment opportunities. The whole discourse on education is set within the context of a continent that has experienced a significant decline in the level of investment in educational sector due to fiscal problems arising from economic recession, structural adjustment programs, and global economic restructuring (Beoku-Betts, 1998). Implementation of structural adjustment policies presents a crisis (Mbilinyi, 1998) that has had an extremely detrimental impact on the education of all children, especially girls. The interplay between the high cost of schooling and the gendered cultural assumptions continue to limit girls' secondary and tertiary educational opportunities while impacting negatively on the health of their mothers. As Beoku-Betts argues, enrollment in the elementary level are misleading. She observes that attainment and accomplishment levels are strong explanatory variables with which to assess the situation of women and girls in Africa.

Finally, factors that shape women's education are as complex as the context within which the education occurs. Women's private discourse on education is one that is delineated by challenges and courage. Many experts on women's education have advocated a working partnership among policy makers, educational institutions, and local communities to alleviate the current situation. Although this strategy might lead toward gender equity in educational opportunities, I feel that sacrifices that mothers make to educate their children are not compensated. The demand for higher credentials, therefore more resources, makes it impossible for women to afford their children the skills required in a competitive labor market. The myth that there are jobs at the end of high school also needs to be demystified. What we need is an education that creates opportunities for self-reliance—a challenge to all.

Chapter 1

1. Women's agency refers to the ability of women to critically examine their situations and to adopt strategies that will address their needs. Also, see Gardner's (1995) edited work on gender and agency in theory and practice.

2. Smith (1987) writes of a standpoint of women not from a feminist standpoint. I prefer the former because it embraces the diversity of women's experiences. Some academics/writers/researchers have tended to "bundle" women (Third World, Black, and white), their experiences, languages, and so forth. Some of this "bundling" or generalization is erroneous, Unfortunately, errors like these are perpetuated to the readership.

3. I analyzed the following documents: the Ominde Report of 1964, the first nonracial educational report in Kenya; Sessional Paper # 10 (1965), African Socialism and Its Application to Planning in Kenya (1965); the Gachathi Report (1976); the MacKay Report (1981); the Wanjigi Report (1982–1983); the Kamunge Report (1988); the Ndegwa Report (1991); 1974–1978 and 1989–1993 national development plans.

4. Structural adjustment policies (SAP) (imposed by the International Monetary Fund [IMF]) have wrought social, economic, and political havoc of an unprecedented scale. George's "A fate worse than debt" (1994) gives an glimpse of the sacrifices that developing countries are making to implement an IMF-mandated structural adjustment program. Also, Mbilinyi (1998) examines the impact of these SAPs on the education of women in Tanzania.

5. While there are similarities in the construction of gender within different contexts, I have come to acknowledge and appreciate their differences.

Ethnicity, culture, and class influence the construction of gender. However, national culture that is shaped by microcultures and economic and political contexts influences the opportunities that are made available to both men and women.

6. Many African/Black feminists and scholars such as hooks (1984), Amadiume (1989), and Stamp (1989) dispute the universality of this private/public dichotomy. I argue that this dichotomy is relevant in understanding the exclusion of women from the public sphere.

Chapter 2

1. The colonial government provided educational and economic opportunities along racial, ethnic, and gender lines. Areas inhabited by the nomadic ethnic groups such as the Maasai, Turkana, and Borana, were totally marginalized. This legacy of economic, educational, political and social marginalization has continued into present-day Kenya.

2. The national enrollment rate is the percentage of enrollment of all school-age children.

3. See Nzomo (1997) for a detailed discussion on women and politics in Kenya.

4. These are the latest statistics available. Later reports do not show enrollment along gender lines in the different types of schools in Kenya.

5. Formal and informal sectors are two contrasting sectors that exist in the economy. The former is more organized and modern in nature. It is characterized by capital intensive technology, high wages for its employees, large-scale operations, and corporate or governmental organization. The latter is mostly unorganized. Traditionally, its employees have less education, and are unskilled and lowly paid. The sector is labor intensive (Women's Bureau/SIDA Projects, 1992).

6. In Kenya the term *graduate* refers to individuals who have completed university level education.

7. Few women can earn any income from traditional beer brewing because it has been made illegal. Illegal brewers, however, do exist. The only person who had the authority to brew traditional beer in Ukambani (the area where data were collected) was the wealthy retired commander of the armed forces, who was also the minister for lands and settlement. This man has been rewarded heavily for crashing the 1982 air force-led coup that threatened to topple the present government.

8. A time came when my mother subtly withdrew her labor and neglected the coffee plants, which later dried up.

Chapter 3

1. This an estimate of the population of Kilome town since there are no official statistics.

2. The labor demands of this crop are high, and women are responsible for its cultivation. Nevertheless, the coffee is registered in the name of the husband as the owner of the plot. Often, women are not signatories to the account held at the cooperative. The few women who mentioned having had coffee pointed out that they were no longer willing to work for nothing because they never saw the fruits of their labor. I met one woman in Kithumba who neglected her husband's "coffee" (as she called it) and concentrated on subsistence crops. She did this because her husband always collected the money from the cooperative to spend it with his other wife. She noted that she could not uproot it because it was not only against the law but she would also be killed by her husband. Stamp (1986) found similar resistance strategies employed by Kikuyu women.

3. Gabions are large baskets made of wire mesh and filled with rocks and soil. They are used to help stop soil erosion.

4. Ambua clan is one of the many clans that make up the Akamba ethnic group. An individual from the Ambua (rainmakers) clan is called a "Muumbua."

Chapter 4

1. I went to Kilome division determined not to be a "fly on the wall." I did not want to be a "tourist researcher"—one who has the courage to write generalized discourses on women based on brief encounters with women in the marketplaces.

2. It is common for schooled people to mix their vernacular with English or Swahili.

Chapter 5

1. This is the ruling party since independence in 1963.

2. The term *African socialism* was used to describe an African political and economic system that is "positively African not being imported from any country or being a blueprint of any foreign ideology but capable of incorporating useful and compatible techniques from whatever source" (Sessional Paper # 10, 1965, pp. 2–3).

Chapter 6

1. Aware that my educational achievements were higher than those of the women, I did not want to begin the discussions by talking about their educational achievements. They would think I was showing off.

2. The education system in Kenya is divided into primary, secondary, and tertiary levels of education. Primary level starts from Standards 1 to 8 and Secondary from Forms 1 to 4.

3. Janet helped her mother with all the household work, although she notes that she "sat at home."

4. In those days, girls would start schooling when they were mature. The aim was to help them to be able to read and reply to letters written to them by their husband.

5. To be admitted to Standard 1 a child must be at least six years old.

Chapter 8

1. This is an Akamba saying that means that you can still be poor but retain your dignity.

2. Kilome division is overpopulated and families have small pieces of land to grow food crops. Unfortunately, the yields are poor and almost all of the families have to buy maize and beans. Mavivye is a market that is situated in an area that was previously reserved for settlers. When the settlers left, families moved in and acquired larger pieces of land where they grow maize and beans and harvest enough to eat and to sell.

3. The latest report I received from Kyandue is that Ngina has stopped working on her plot because her health has deteriorated. She was recently admitted into a hospital in critical condition.

Chapter 9

1. *Kuasan'ya* is not the equivalent of "paying" bridewealth. The Kamba word for "paying" is *kuiva* or *kuthooa,* which is different from *kuasan'ya.*

2. When a woman gave birth, she wrapped her abdomen with a special type of rope. The rope was used to support and to strengthen the stomach muscles.

3. A borehole is a deep well that is drilled using drilling machines.

Chapter 10

1. The formal sector in Kenya is made up of the public and the private sectors.

2. A recent case in mind is the threat uttered by a Mr. Chepkok, a member of parliament to Wangari Mathai-Founder of the GreenBelt movement in Kenya, in which he threatened that if she visited his constituency against his wish, she would be circumcised Kalenjin style—the ethnic group to which Chepkok belongs.

Bibliography

Ahlberg-Maina, Beth. (1991). *Women, sexuality, and the changing social order: The impact of government policies on reproductive behavior in Kenya*. Philadelphia: Gordon and Breach.

Alcoff, Linda. (Winter 1991–1992). The problem of speaking for others. *Cultural critique 23*, 5–31.

Amadiume, I. (1989). *Male daughters and female husbands: Gender and sex in an African society*. London: Zed Books.

Anderson, K., and D. C. Jack. (1991). Learning to listen: Interview techniques and analyses. In S. B. Gluck and D. Patai (eds.), *Women's words: The feminist practice of oral history*. New York: Routledge.

Apple, M. (1991). Series editor's introduction. In P. Lather, *Getting smart feminist research and pegagogy with/in the postmodern* (pp. vii–xi). New York: Routledge.

Ardener, S. (1975). "Sexual insult and female militancy," In S. Ardener (ed.), *Perveiving women* (pp. 29–54). New York: Halsted Press.

Bell, D., P. Caplan, and W. H. Karim. (eds.). (1993). *Gendered fields: Women, men and ethnography*. New York: Routledge.

Bellew, R. T., and E. King. (1993). Educating women: Lessons from experience. in E. King and M. A. Hills (eds.), *Women's education in developing countries: Barrier, benefits, and policies*. Baltimore: Johns Hopkins University Press.

Beoku-Betts, J. (1998). Gender and formal education in Africa: An exploration of the opportunity structure at the secondary and tertiary levels. In M. Bloch, J. A. Beoku-Betts, and B. R. Tabachnick (eds.), *Women and education in sub-Saharan Africa: Power, opportunities, and constraints* (pp. 157–184). Boulder, CO: Lynne Rienner Publishers.

Biraimah, K. (1991). Access, equity, and course outcomes: Women students' participation in Nigerian higher education. In G. P. Kelly and S. Slaughter (eds.), *Women's higher education in comparative perspective* (pp. 219–231). Netherlands: Kluwer Academic Publishers.

Bloch, M., and F. Vavrus. (1998). Gender and educational research, policy, and practice in sub-Saharan Africa: Theoretical and empirical problems and prospects. In M. Bloch, J. A. Beoku-Betts, and B. R. Tabachnick (eds.), *Women and education in sub-Saharan Africa: Power, opportunities and constraints* (pp. 1–24). London: Lynne Rienner Publishers.

Boserup, E. (1970). *Women's role in economic development*. London: George Allen and Unwin.

Bradshaw, W., R. Noonan, L. Gash, and C. B. Shershe. (1993). Borrowing against the future: Children and Third World indebtedness. *Social Forces 71* (3). 629–657.

Brett, E. A. (1983). The world's view of the IMF. In *The poverty brokers: The IMF and Latin America*. London: Latin America Bureau.

Children and women in Kenya: A situation analysis. (1992). A publication of the Government of Kenya and the UNICEF Kenya Country Office: Nairobi: Reata Printers.

Chlebowska, K. (1990). *Literacy for rural women in the Third World*. Paris: UNESCO.

Cubbins, L. A. (1991). Women, men, and the division of power: A study of gender stratification in Kenya. *Social Forces, 69* (4), 1063–1083.

Dale, R. (1989). *The state and education policy*. Toronto: OISE Press.

Davies, B. C. (1986). Introduction: Feminist consciousness and African literary criticism. In C. B. Davies and A. A. Graves (eds.), *Ngambika studies of women in African literature* (pp. 1–24). Trenton, NJ: African World Press.

Dei, G. J. S. (1995). *Indigenous knowledge and social development: Making connections*. Invitational address read at the International Development Organizations Conference. York University, Ontario, 3–5 February.

Downey, L. W. (1988). *Policy analysis in education*. Calgary, CAN: Detselig Enterprises.

D'Oyley, V. R., and C. E. Lewis. (1998). C. E. Lewis (ed.). *Re/visioning: Canadian perspectives on the education of Africans in the late twentieth Century*. North York, ONT: Cactus Press.

Due, J. (1991). Policies to overcome the negative effects of structural adjustment programs on African female-headed households. In C. H.

Gladwin (ed.), *Structural adjustment and African women farmers.* Gainesville: University of Florida Press.

Dworkin, D. L., and L. G. Roman. (1993). *Views beyond the border country: Raymond Williams and cultural politics.* New York: Routledge.

Eichler, M. (1983). *Sexism in research and its policy implications.* Ottawa, ONT: CRIAW.

Eshiwani, G. S. (1983). *"A study of women's access to higher education in Kenya with special reference to mathematics and science education."* Unpublished report. Nairobi: Bureau of Educational Research.

————. (1985). The education of women in Kenya, 1975–1984 (ERIC Document Reproduction Service No. ED 284 802).

————. (1990). *Implementing educational policies in Kenya.* World Bank discussion papers. Africa Technical Department Series. Washington, DC: World Bank.

Eyre, L. (1993). "The social construction of gender in the practical arts." Unpublished doctoral dissertation, University of British Columbia, Vancouver.

Fals-Borda, O., and A. M. Rahman. (eds.). (1991). *Action and knowledge: Breaking the monopoly with participatory action-research.* New York: Apex Press.

Feldman, Rayah. (1983). Women's groups subordination: An analysis of policies towards rural women in Kenya. *Review of African Political Economy 27–28*, 67–85.

Foucault, M. (1980b). Power/Knowledge: Selected interviews and other writings 1972–1977. New York: Pantheon Books.

Freeman, C. (1988). Colonialism and the formation of gender hierarchies in Kenya. *Critique of anthropology 7* (3), 33–50.

Freire, P. (1985). *The politics of education: Culture, power, and liberation.* Massachusetts: Bergin and Garvey.

————. (1990). *Pedagogy of the oppressed (3rd ed.).* New York: Continuum Publishing Company.

Gachathi Report. (1976). *Report of the national committee on educational objectives.* Republic of Kenya. Nairobi: Government Printers.

Gardiner, J. K. (ed.). (1995). *Provoking agents: Gender and agency in theory and practice* (pp. 133–151). Chicago: University of Illinois Press.

George, S. (1994). *A fate worse than debt: A radical analysis of the Third World debt crisis.* Toronto, ONT: Penguin Group.

Gluck, S. B., and D. Patai (eds.). (1991). *Women's words: The feminist practice of oral history.* New York: Routledge.

Gruduah, O. (December 1991). When the going gets tough the dynamic Wangari gets tough. *Standard,* 15.

Hakansson, T. (1988). *Bridewealth, women, and land: Social change among the Gusii of Kenya.* Stockholm: Graphic Systems.

Hammersley, M., and P. Atkison. (1983). *Ethnography principles and practice.* New York: Tavistock Publications.

Harding, S. (ed.). (1986). *Feminism and methodology: Social science issues.* Bloomington: Indiana University Press.

Hartmann, H. I. (1993). The unhappy marriage of marxism and feminism: Towards a more progressive union. In A. M. Jaggar and P. S. Rothenberg (eds.), *Feminist frameworks: Alternative theoretical accounts of the relations between men and women* (3rd ed.), (pp. 191–202). New York: McGraw-Hill.

Hill, M. J. (1991). *The harambee movement in Kenya: Self-help, development, and education among the Kamba of Kitui district.* Atlantic Highlands, NJ: Athlone Press.

hooks, b. (1984). Feminist theory from margin to center. Boston: South End Press.

House-Midamba, B. (1996). Gender, democratization, and associational life in Kenya. (Reconceptualizing African Women: Toward the Year 2000). *Africa Today 43* (3), 289–306.

Hughes, R., and K. Mwiria. (1989). Kenyan women, higher education, and the labour market. *Comparative Education 25* (2), 179–195.

Hyde, K. (1993). Sub-Saharan Africa. In E. M. King and M. A. Hill (eds.), *Women's education in developing countries: Barriers, benefits, and policies.* Baltimore: Johns Hopkins University Press.

International Labour Organization (ILO). (1991). *Exploratory mission on women's employment.* ILO, Geneva.

Jaggar, A. (1983). *Feminist politics and human nature.* Totowa, NJ: Rowman & Littlefield Publishers.

Jobs and skills programme for Africa (JASPA). (1981). *Employment problems of rural women in Kenya.* International Labour Office. Addis Ababa, ETH.

———. (1986). *Women's employment patterns, discrimination, and promotion of equality in Kenya.* International Labour Office. Addis Ababa, ETH.

Kagia, R. (1985). The effect of education on employment opportunities for women in Kenya. In N. Olembo, E. Gachukia, and N. Waita (eds.), *Kenyan women in development: Research papers for forum 1985.* Nairobi.

Kamunge Report. (1988). Republic of Kenya. *Report on the presidential working party on education and manpower training for the next decade and beyond.* Nairobi: Government Printers.

Kardam, Nuket. (1991). *Bringing women in: Women's issues in international development programs.* London: Lynne Rienner Publishers.

Kibwana, K. (1992). Gender and development: Why gender is a development issue. A discussion paper prepared for CREUMHS' *Gender awareness workshop for Kwale water project personnel.* Mombasa, KEN.

Kiiti, N. (December 1993). Swimming against the current: Maintaining a balance between building a successful career and making home is a stressful exercise. *Lady,* pp. 17–18.

King, E. M., and A. M. Hill (eds.). (1993). *Women's education in developing countries: Barriers, benefits, and policies.* Baltimore, MD: Johns Hopkins University Press.

Kinnear, K. (1997). *Women in the Third World: A refence handbook.* Santa Barbara, CA: ABC-CLIO.

Lather, P. (1991). *Feminist research in education: Within/against.* Victoria, CAN: Deakin University.

———. (1986). Issues of validity in openly ideological research: Between a rock and a soft place. *Interchange, 17* (4), 63–84.

Llewelyn-Davies, M. (1981). Women, warriors, and patriarchs. In S. B. Ortner and H. Whitehead (eds.), *Sexual meanings: The construction of gender and sexuality* (pp. 330–358). London: Cambridge University Press.

MacKay Report. (1981). *Second university in Kenya.* Republic of Kenya. Nairobi: Government Printers.

Mann, S. P. (1995). Cyborgean motherhood and abortion. In J. K. Gardiner (ed.), *Provoking agents: Gender and agency in theory and practice* (pp. 133–151). Chicago: University of Illinois Press.

Mbataru, W. (1999, May). Feeding programme keeps girls in school. *The Nation,* p. 1.

Mbilinyi, M. (1972). The "new woman" and traditional norms in Tanzania. *Journal of Modern African Studies 10* (1), 57–72.

———. (1998). Searching for utopia: The politics of gender and education in Tanzania. In M. Bloch, J. A. Beoku-Betts, and B. Tabachnick (eds.), *Women and education in sub-Saharan Africa: Power, opportunities, and constraints* (pp. 277–298). Boulder, CO: Lynne Rienner Publishers.

Mbiti, J. S. (1990). *African religions and philosophy* (2nd ed.). Portsmouth, NH: Heinemann.

McAdoo, P. H., and M. Were. (1987). Extended family involvement and roles of urban Kenyan women. In R. Terborg-Penn, S. Harley, and A. Rushing (eds.), *Women in Africa and African diaspora*. Washington, DC: Howard University Press.

Mies, M. (1983). Towards a methodology for feminist research. In G. Bowles and R. Klein (eds.), *Theories of women's studies*. London: Routledge & Kegan Paul.

Mikell, G. (ed.). (1997). *African feminism: The politics of survival in sub-Saharan Africa*. Philadelphia: University of Pennsylvania Press.

Mohanty, C. (1991). Under western eyes: Feminist scholarship and colonial discourses. In C. Mohanty, A. Russo, and L. Torres (eds.), *Third World women and the politics of feminism* (pp. 51–80). Indianapolis: Indiana University Press.

Mukui, J. T. (1985). The impact of social factors on the employment situation of women in Kenya. In N. Olembo, E. Gachukia, and N. Waita (eds.), *Kenyan women in development: Research papers for forum 1985*. Nairobi.

Munachonga, M. (1988). Income allocation and marriage options in urban Zambia. In D. Dwyer and J. Bruce (eds.), *A home divided: Women and income in the Third World* (pp. 173–194). Stanford, CA: Stanford University Press.

Muthiani, J. (1973). *Akamba from within: Egalitarianism in social relations*. New York: Exposition Press.

Nation Writer. (November 1999). Main culprits in Kenya's poverty creation league. *Nation*, 5.

Ndegwa Report. (1991). Republic of Kenya. *Development and employment in Kenya: A strategy for the transformation of the economy*. Nairobi: Government Printers.

Ndunda, M., and H. Munby. (1991). "Because I am a woman": A study of culture, school, and futures in science. *Science Education 75* (6), 683–699.

Nzomo, M. (1989). The impact of the Women's Decade on policies, programs, and empowerment of women in Kenya. *Issue, 17* (2), 8–16.

———. (1997). Kenyan women in politics. In M. Gwendolyn (ed.), *African feminism: The politics of survival in sub-Saharan Africa* (pp. 232–256). Philadelphia: University of Pennsylvania Press.

Obbo, C. (1980). *African women: Their struggle for economic independence*. London: Zed Press.

Obura, A. (1992). *Changing images: Portrayal of girls and women in Kenyan textbooks*. Nairobi: ACTS Press.

Odiege, P. O. (1992). Local coping strategies in Machakos district, Kenya. In F. D. Taylor and F. Mackenzie (eds.), *Development from within: Survival in rural Africa*. New York: Routledge.

Ominde, H. (1964). *Kenya Education Commission Report*. Nairobi: Government Printers.

Ortner, S. (1981). Accounting for sexual meanings. In S. Ortner and Whitehead (eds.), *Sexual meanings: The cultural construction of gender and sexuality*. Cambridge: Cambridge University Press.

Osler, A. (1993). Education for development and democracy in Kenya: A case study. *Educational Review 45* (2), 165–173.

Peattie, L. R. (1981). *Thinking about development*. New York: Plenum Press.

Potash, B. (1989). Gender relations in sub-Saharan Africa. *Gender and anthropology critical reviews for research and teaching*. Washington, DC: American Anthropological Association.

Rathgeber, E. (1991). Women in higher education in Africa: Access and choices. In G. P. Kelly and S. Slaughter (eds.), *Women's higher education in comparative perspective* (pp. 47–62). Netherlands: Kluwer Academic Publishers.

Reinharz, S. (1992). *Feminist methods in social research*. Toronto: ONT: Oxford University Press.

Republic of Kenya. *1974–1978 development plan*. Nairobi: Government Printers.

———. *Laws of Kenya: Education act (1980)*. Nairobi: Government Printers.

———. *1989–1993 national development plan*. Nairobi: Government Printers.

Republic of Kenya. *Statistical abstracts (1991)*. Central Bureau of Statistics, Ministry of Planning and National Development. Nairobi: Government Printers.

———. *Development and employment report, 1991*. Nairobi: Government Printers.

———. *Economic survey, 1990*. Ministry of Planning and National Development. Nairobi: Central Bureau of Statistics.

———. *Economic survey, 1991*. Ministry of Planning and National Development. Nairobi: Central Bureau of Statistics.

———. *Kanu manifesto sessional paper # 10, 1965*. African socialism and its application to planning in Kenya. Nairobi: Government Printers.

———. Ministry of Labour. (1968). *Helping you choose a career*. Kenyanization of Personnel Bureau. Nairobi: Government Printers.

————. Statistical abstracts. (1991). Nairobi: Government Printers.

————. *Employment and earnings in the formal and informal sector: A gender analysis*. Women's Bureau/SIDA Project, 1993. Ministry of Culture and Social Services. Nairobi: Government Printers.

Riria-Ouko, J. (1984). Education for all: The neglected half. *Basic education resource centre*. Nairobi.

Robertson, C., and I. Berger (eds.). (1986). *Women and class in Africa*. New York: Africana Publishing Company.

Salazar, C. (1991). A Third World woman's text: Between the politics of criticism and cultural politics. In S. B. Gluck and D. Patai (eds.), *Women's words: The feminist practice of oral history* (pp. 93–106). New York: Routledge.

Scheurich, J. (1997). *Research method in the postmodern*. Washington, DC: Falmer Press.

Scott, M. A. (1990). Patterns of patriarchy in the Peruvian working class. In S. Stichter and J. L. Parpart (eds.), *Women, employment, and the family in the international division of labour* (pp. 198–220). Hampshire, ENG: Macmillan Press.

Sifuna, N. D. (1990). *Development of education in Africa: The Kenyan experience*. Nairobi: Initiatives.

Smith, D. E. (1987). *Everyday world as problematic: A feminist sociology*. Toronto: University of Toronto Press.

Stacey, J. (1991). Can there be a feminist ethnography? In S. B. Gluck and D. Patai (eds.), *Women's words: The feminist practice of oral history*. New York: Routledge.

Stackhouse, J. (March 9, 1995). Why land is better than a job. World Watch, *Globe & Mail*.

Stambach, A. (1998). "Education is my husband": Marriage, gender, and reproduction in northern Tanzania. In, M. Bloch, J. A. Beoku-Betts, and B. R. Tabachnick (eds.), *Women and education in sub-Saharan Africa: Power, opportunities, and constraints* (pp. 185–200). Boulder, CO: Lynne Rienner Publishers.

Stamp, P. (1986). Kikuyu women's self-help groups: Toward an understanding of the relation between sex-gender system and mode of production in Africa. In C. Robertson and I. Berger. (eds.), *Women and class in Africa* (pp. 27–47). New York: Africana Publishing Company.

————. (1989). *Technology, gender, and power in Africa*. Ottawa, ONT: IDRC.

———. (1991). Burying Otieno: The politics of gender and ethnicity. *Signs* *16* (4), 808–845.

———. (1995). Mothers of invention: Women's agency in the Kenyan state. In L. Gardner (ed.), *Provoking agents, gender, and agency in theory and practice* (pp. 69–92). Chicago: University of Illinois Press.

Staudt, K. (1987). Women's politics, the state, and capitalist transformation in African. In I. L. Markovitz (ed.), *Studies in power and class in Africa* (pp. 193–208). New York: Oxford University Press.

Staudt, K., and H. Glickman. (1989). Beyond Nairobi: Women's politics and policies in Africa revisited. *Issue: Journal of Opinion 17* (2), 4–7.

Staudt, K., and J. Parpart. (1989). Introduction to women and the state in Africa. In K. Staudt and J. Parpart (eds.), *Women and the state in Africa* (pp. 1–19). Boulder, CO: Lynne Rienner Publishers.

Stichter, S. (1982). *Migrant labor in Kenya: Capitalism and African response, 1895–1975.* Essex, UK: Longman.

Stichter, S., and L. J. Parpart. (1988). *Patriarchy and class: African women in the home and the workforce.* Boulder, CO: Westview Press.

Stromquist, N. P. (1987). Global perspectives on sexuality and equity in education. *Peabody journal of education 64* (4), 25–43.

———. (1991). Feminist reflections on the Peruvian university politics. In G. P. Kelly and S. Slaughter (eds.), *Women's higher education in comparative perspective* (pp. 63–83). Netherlands: Kluwer Academic Publishers.

Thomas, B. (1985). *Politics, participation and poverty: Development through self-help in Kenya.* Boulder, CO: Westview Press.

Thomas, R. M. (ed.). (1992). *Education's role in national development plans: Ten country cases.* New York: Praeger.

UNICEF. (1992). *Strategies to promote girls' education: Policies and programmes that work.* Education Section. New York: UNICEF.

———. (1993). *The "lesser child."* Nairobi.

United Nations Children's Fund (UNICEF). 1989. *The state of the world's children, 1989.* Oxford University Press.

Urdvardy, M. (1988). Women's groups near the Kenyan coast: Patron-clientship in the development arena. In D. W. Brokensha and P. D. Little (eds.), *Anthropology of development and change in East Africa* (pp. 217–237). Boulder, CO: Westview Press.

Van Allen, J. (1976). "Aba riots" or Igbo "women's war"? Ideology, stratification, and the invisibility of women. In N. Hafkin and E. Bay (eds.),

Women in Africa: Studies in social and economic change. Stanford, CA: Stanford University Press.

Van Maanen, J. (1988). *Tales of the field.* Chicago: University of Chicago Press.

Vickers, J. (1991). *Women and the world economic crisis.* Gordonville, NJ: Saint Martin's Press.

Wanjigi Report. (1982–1983). *Unemployment report.* Republic of Kenya. Nairobi: Government Printers.

WIN News. (Spring 1995). *World Bank structural adjustment and gender.*

Wipper, A. (1995). Women's voluntary associations. In M. J. Hay and S. Stichter (eds.), *African women south of the Sahara* (pp. 164–186). New York: John Wiley & Sons.

World Bank Country Study, Kenya. (1989). *The role of women in economic development.* Washington, DC: World Bank.

Yunus, M. (March 5, 1991). [Interview with David Cayley, Ideas writer *CBC: The Grameen Bank*]. CBC IDEAS Transcripts.

Index

Scott, 120
Serchen, 139
Sessional Paper #10, 61, 62, 63,
76, 167, 175
sex education
responsibility, 112–114
schools and communities, 169
sexuality, 50, 114, 169
Sifuna, 84
Smith, 44, 173
society, traditional and modern, 65
Stacey, 48, 49
Stambach, 158
Stamp, 13, 17, 18, 19, 20, 21, 40,
42, 43, 44, 45, 142, 153, 154,
166, 171, 174
Staudt, 23, 84, 156, 158, 161, 162,
166, 167, 175
Stichter, 14, 18, 126
Stromquist, 98,
structural adjustments programs,
102
cost-sharing strategy, 3, 10, 63,
71, 72, 77, 104, 120, 139, 161,
163
implementation, 103, 124, 135,
141
policies, 98, 103, 163
Sub Saharan Africa, 169
Summary Report, 80–81

Thomas, 20, 56, 57

unemployment, 78
UNICEF/GOK, 7, 11, 21, 131, 138,
142, 146, 168
United Nations Declaration, women's
decade (1975–1985), 78
Urdvardy, 33, 146

Van Allen, 41, 48
Vavrus, 7, 120
vocationalization
masonry, 68
self-employment, 68

subjects, 163
tailoring, 68

Wanjigi Report, 57, 58, 69, 70, 76,
77, 162
Were, 17
Win News, 124
Wipper, 142
women
Ambua, 31
careers, 18, 22
children, challenge to educate,
102–103, 134, 137
discrimination, 85
dominance and exploitation, 18, 85
economic activities, 70; Kilome,
119
economic agents, 78, 85
education and economic opportunities, 66
exclusion of rural, 52,
family life, 17
gender roles, 67, 85
income generating opportunities,
75, 93, 96, 128, 160; petty
business, 133–134; sacrifice,
132
motherhood, 17, 18, 109, 111
peasants, 19
political power, 22
professional women, 109;
motherhood, 125
resistance, 46
responsibilities, 66, 87
sacrifices, 155
self-help groups, 20
social actors, 43, 171
standpoints, 39, 44
status, 66
subordination, 2
supermothers, 45
underrepresentation of, 78
women's
decade (1975–1985). *See* United
Nations Declaration
health, 135–137